GLADIATOR

GLADIATOR

WITCHCRAFT, PROPAGANDA, AND THE RISE OF THE WORLD HERO

JOHN D. CHRISTIAN

RCP RiverCrest Publishing
1708 Patterson Road · Austin, Texas 78733

Originally published by Underground Press,
New Zealand

Acknowledgement:

Special thanks to brother E. Christian for his
gracious comments, advice and editing contribution
to this book.

All scriptures quoted in this book are from the
Authorized King James Version.

Cover design: Sandra Myers

Art on the front cover is from the guilded and engraved Parabiago
plate, found in northern Italy, from around the fourth century.

Printed in the United States of America

Library of Congress Catalog Card Number 2001117994

Categories: 1. Religion-Bible Prophecy   2. Occultism
              3. Current Affairs   4. Performing Arts

ISBN 1-930004-09-5

DEDICATION

To the valiant martyrs of Jesus Christ, the true heroes of the Roman Colosseum, **who provided the seeds of the Church** *by their own blood and amazing testimony of faith.*

To the martyrs of Christ, in the future, who may very well close the Christian era with their own blood, like their early Church brethren who opened it at its epoch, on the sands of their own local "Roman sports stadiums."

HOLY BIBLE
[King James Version]

Matthew 24:4—And Jesus answered and said unto them, **TAKE HEED THAT NO MAN DECEIVE YOU.**

Matthew 24:24—For there shall arise false Christs, and false prophets, and shall shew great signs and wonders; insomuch that, **IF IT WERE POSSIBLE, THEY SHALL DECEIVE THE <u>VERY</u> ELECT.**

Revelation 12:9—And the great dragon, was cast out, that old serpent, called the Devil, and Satan, <u>**WHICH DECEIVETH THE WHOLE WORLD:**</u> *he was cast out into the earth, and his angels were cast out with him.*

CONTENTS

BLOOD GAMES, THE 21ST CENTURY CHRISTIAN, AND THE GLADIATOR

Is it possible that significantly important, hidden messages permeate many of our movies today? Could it be that through the unique cultural medium of cinema, hundreds of millions of unsuspecting viewers are being hypnotized and programmed without their knowledge—being prepared for a future age of Big Brother and made ready to accept the most heinous evil to come?

That is the contention of John D. Christian in this thought-provoking and insightful book, *Gladiator*. The title, of course, refers to the Ridley Scott-directed movie, *Gladiator*, an Academy Award-winning film which won Oscars both for Best Movie of the year and Best Actor (Russell Crowe).

Mr. Christian is persuaded by voluminous evidence—which he presents to readers in the pages which follow—that *Gladiator* is a movie that attempts to revise and rewrite true history. More ominous, however, he expresses his firm conviction that this much lauded and critically received film is, in fact, a masterpiece of satanic propaganda, designed to implant in the minds of viewers a message which is a call to worship the coming prophesied Antichrist of the Holy Bible's Book of Revelation.

If the author is correct, then we can expect the movie *Gladiator* to be imbued with very special supernatural powers to mesmerize and deceive. Certainly, the history of our planet reveals that this movie would not be the first to be endowed with such unusual powers to influence the minds of men, women, and children.

A Masterpiece of Propaganda

Mr. Christian, this book's author, presents documentation that the movie studio which produced the *Gladiator* epic actually admits in one of its own publications that the movie is patterned after what is arguably considered to be the 20th century's greatest mind control cinematic production, the celebrated Hitlerian documentary, *Triumph of The Will*, directed by famous German photographer Leni Reinfenstahl. In a separate book accompanying the movie, *Gladiator*, its makers reveal:

> "(Director) Ridley Scott wanted Commodus's grand entrance into Rome to echo Nazi-era propaganda films like Leni Reifenstahl's Triumph of The Will."

We cannot, based on the present evidence, maintain with certainty that its director or producers desired their acclaimed movie, *Gladiator*, to be endowed with monumental satanic powers to program and channel men's minds and energies in the direction of evil. But such a purpose cannot be ruled out. It has been my observation that many, many men and women in a variety of professions—from architects to artists, authors, medical doctors, and movie producers—are being led, often without their conscious knowledge, into wicked paths in order to influence the masses.

Possibly, this is also true of movie director Ridley Scott and others involved in the making of *Gladiator*. Oftentimes, those who provide Satan with the most magnificent service are wholly unaware that their talents are being used for evil. That is the tragedy of unregenerated man and his modern culture.

Subversive Movies

In a recent edition of *The Lofton Letter*, my friend, the astute commentator John Lofton, wrote of how one particular classic Hollywood movie was originally produced with the specific intent of effecting societal change through the implantation of certain religious images, motives and goals. Lofton related:

> There I was watching cable TV ("American Movie Classics"), a program called "Backstory" which gives us inside info about how a movie was made. The particular flick this night is one of my favorites, the 1951 classic, *The Day The Earth Stood Still*.
>
> OK. So, midway through this show, we're told there was a "sneaky, subversive subtext" in this film, with parallels

between the peace-loving alien (actor Michael Rennie, robot "Gort's" boss) and—Jesus Christ!" How so? Well, Rennie's character, at one point, calls himself "Mr. Carpenter." Also, he dies and is resurrected.

But, says the narrator, the alien's power over life and death did not slip past censors "who insisted the blasphemous plot-point be changed." It was. In a re-take, when asked if he had the power to create eternal life, the alien says no, only for a short period of time. Re: the eternal life power, the alien says: "That power is reserved to the Almighty Spirit. This technique, in some cases, can restore life for a limited power."

At another point, Forrest J. Ackerman, a magazine editor/ archivist, says of this movie, approvingly: "We didn't have a man and his robot come here to rule the world. He came here to warn us we better straighten up and fly right or we're going to fly right out of the solar system and be burned to a cinder. It was nice for a change to have a very charismatic individual from another world rather than a villainous one."

Nick Redman, a film historian, says this movie "revealed to the audience a truth that had been hidden from them which was to put our fears and phobias and hysteria to one side and learn to love one another."

Director Robert Wise says of his film: "I think it was a very important message that we all believe in very much: Let's stop fighting and having these wars." Co-star Patricia Neal says *The Day The Earth Stood Still* was "a divine film."

Well, now. Speaking of the "divine," some of this sounds
very familiar. A warning from someone not of this world
to shape up or be scorched? A preacher of a hidden truth
by a charismatic person calling for, among other things,
love? No more wars?

Hmmmmm. Sounds a little like the Lord Jesus Christ, no?

Lofton's illustration is proven over and over again
in movies ranging from _ET_ to _Bladerunner_. Man is
depicted to be his own god, and aliens from outer space
or another dimension or parallel universe are his teachers
and benefactors.

An Unquenchable Passion for Blood and Death

The movie _Gladiator_ does not press these same claims
of humans as deity. Its plot and images appear to have
other goals in mind, including possibly the revival of
giving reverence to and worshipping the ancient
gods and goddesses of Rome and Greece. Moreover,
Gladiator appeals to the 21st century's unquenchable
passion for thrills, blood, carnage, violence, brutality,
and death!

Clif Droke, publisher of _Last Days Journal_, made
note of this moral aberration and inhumane tendency on
the part of modern society recently when he wrote:

> The one central theme characterizing man's dealings in
> these last days is bloodlust... Blood is a theme that
> permeates the lyrics of nearly all forms of popular
> music—rock, heavy metal, rap. It is evident in popular

movies and in television programs, comic books, video games, and internet sites.

The Wall Street Journal (Aug. 7, 1997), carried an article entitled, "Blood On The Net: Computer Games See Red." The article described a burgeoning gaming industry for teenagers and young adults who favor games with bloody, violent themes. Advertisements for these latest games are said to "ooze with blood: Young men are shown bathing in tubs of it; warriors clutch dripping human hearts." One game features a sporty red speedster with an "optional hood ornament"—a screaming, bloodied pedestrian.

Gladiatorworld

It was not surprising, then, that it was recently announced that an amusement park featuring the blood games based on the movie *Gladiator* would soon be opened. We are graduating from Disneyworld to Gladiatorworld in entertainment interest by the public. In the *New Zealand Herald* newspaper (May 15, 2001), an article announced exactly this amazing development:

Gladiator fights, chariot races, and the torturing of Christian slaves in a lion-filled arena are poised for a comeback more than 1600 years after the fall of the Roman Empire.

The spectacles will take place in France, in a massive, purpose-built arena inspired by the Colosseum in Rome, where some of the bloodiest scenes in Roman history took place.

But if all goes well, any blood on the sand will be fake, for the gory thrills are part of an amusement park in western France, the Grand Parc, to cash in on the excitement generated in Europe by the Hollywood toga epic, *Gladiator*...

The Grand Parc claims the stadium will be a "jaw-droppingly" exciting recreation of a real Roman arena... seven lions and tigers will prowl...

Imagine! The new *Gladiator* amusement theme park is being opened in the very same country, France, in which, only a couple of centuries ago, real blood games were held, with thousands of innocent victims' heads chopped off by the guillotine as chanting and roaring mobs raged with approval. Many of the suffering victims were guilty of only one crime—they were Christians!

Were these bloodlust mobs and onlookers in 18th century revolutionary France any different than the blood-crazed crowds who sat in the Colosseum in Rome and in arenas thoughout the Roman Empire centuries earlier?

Could it be that the Christians who were sacrificed in the Roman arenas and those who were tortured and murdered in the cities of France by guillotine and other heinous methods will be joined by 21st Christians? It seems too preposterous to contemplate.

Surely, one might object, mankind has acquired greater compassion and sensitivity in the intervening years. "Surely," the cheery optimist objects, "modern man could not be induced to commit such atrocities. Not today. Not in America. Not on a civilized Planet Earth!"

Spirit of Bloodlust

But, in fact, the monstrous horrors of 1940s Nazi Germany, 1917-1986 Communist Soviet Russia, 1980s Khmer Rouge Cambodia, and, surprisingly, the first decade of 21st century America, demonstrate that the spirit of bloodlust lives on, unquenched, destructive. Indeed, the federal authorities of the United States proved this same satanic spirit of bloodgames thrives in their murderous attack on Ruby Ridge, their siege, torture and burning to death of 83 innocent men, women and children in Waco, Texas, and their complicity in the bloody bombings of the World Trade Center and the Murrah Federal Building in Oklahoma City, Oklahoma.

"What!" you exclaim, "Are you saying that the federal government lawmen and the elite were either involved in or masterminded the horrors of the World Trade Center and Oklahoma City bombings?" Again, popular culture and entertainment provide the startling answer.

Take, for example, the carnage in Oklahoma City. Did Oklahoma Governor Frank Keating help to coverup the awful truth of government involvement in the "terrorist" bloodletting in his state? In fact, the evidence is staggering that the answer is, *yes*. The object of the Oklahoma City bombing by the government was to conduct a prescribed "Blood Game" to anger and excite the American public against a designated enemy: patriots, nationalists, and militia. Keating's state of Oklahoma presumably was chosen because the Governor formerly had been an FBI agent and also once had served as Assistant Secretary of the Treasury in Washington, D.C., supervising the Secret Service, U.S. Customs Service, and the notorious and murderous Bureau of Alcohol,

Tobacco, and Firearms (ATF). Other members of the Keating clan were active in government intelligence.

Now comes the shocker! Is it just a curious coincidence that the Governor's own brother, Martin Keating, authored a manuscript for a novel in 1991, four years before the actual Oklahoma City bombing and slaughter, which amazingly foresaw key events of the terrorist act? The manuscript by Martin Keating, titled *The Final Jihad*, had for its plot an account of terrorists, based in Oklahoma City, who decide to bomb a federal building. And the name of one of the terrorists in Keating's book is—get this—a "Tom McVey!" That's right, Tom McVey.

Now for the clincher: In *The Final Jihad*, this supposedly fictional novel by Keating, the terrorists are apprehended when their car is stopped by an Oklahoma highway patrolman for a broken taillight. This, of course, we are told by the FBI, is remarkably similar to how the real Tim McVeigh was caught.

Was Martin Keating's manuscript secretly used by the federal authorities as the blueprint for their undercover "Blood Game" project—the bombing of the Oklahoma City federal building and its massive loss of life? It should be noted that actual victims were *not* law enforcement agents but little children and lower-level government workers—administrative clerks, social security employees, postal sorters, etc.

Was the real Timothy McVeigh simply a hapless patsy, the same kind of patsy as was luckless Lee Harvey Oswald some four decades prior?

Moreover, was the slaughter of 168 men, women and children in Oklahoma City carried out according to a preapproved "movie script?" I was not surprised to hear recently that CBS-TV is planning a dramatic miniseries based on the bombing and on the execution by lethal injection of designated patsy, Tim McVeigh (aka Tom McVey?)

A Blood Games Agenda—The Report From Iron Mountain

It is even quite likely that the Oklahoma City atrocity— as well as many other recent historical "terrorist acts" and the whole array of bloody movies and popular modern entertainment, full of violent, blood-soaked, sadistic acts, death and destruction—is all part and parcel of a Blood Games agenda. This deadly agenda has been foisted on the American people and, indeed, on the inhabitants of the entire planet.

In 1963, a special Top Secret commission of government experts met secretly underground in a place called Iron Mountain, a highly protected and shielded defense installation deep inside the earth in New York state. Its mission: To devise goals for the worlds' governments to pursue to insure *continuing control of the people of Earth*, once the Cold War of the two superpowers is ended and global peace ensues.

It was believed by our hidden rulers that wars had been tremendously effective in channeling the peoples energies and permitting governments to establish and maintain social control (pretexts: for state security and defense needs, to present a common front against the enemy, protect the people's way of life, etc.).

If however, wars were abolished, the committee's task was to come up with *alternative mechanisms and methods of social control.*

In its final report to the President of the United States, informally entitled *The Report From Iron Mountain*, the distinguished men of this committee presented five substitutes for war in the event the world's rulers chose to establish a New World Order based on peace and cooperation among the world's superpowers. The substitute for war which stands out from among the others is: *"Blood Games."*

I have in my files a copy of *The Report From Iron Mountain*, and I am astonished at the blunt proposals of this Top Secret committee. Obviously, the government and its hidden rulers never thought for a moment you and I would have access to this classified information, but here it is, from page 71:

> When it comes to postulating a credible substitute for war capable of directing human behavior patterns in behalf of social organizations...the motivational function of war requires a genuinely menacing social enemy...The "alternate enemy" must imply a more immediate, tangible, and directly felt threat of destruction. It must justify the need for taking and paying a "blood price" in wide areas of human concern...

> Games theorists have suggested, in other contexts, the development of *"Blood Games"* for effective control of individual aggressive impulses... It was left to the makers of a commercial film, *The Tenth Victim*, to develop a model for this...on the implausible level of popular melodrama, as a ritualized manhunt.

> More realistically, such a (Blood Games) ritual might be socialized, in the manner of the Spanish Inquisition and

the less formal witch trials of other periods, for purposes of "social purification," "state security," or other rationale both acceptable and credible to postwar societies.

The high-level government intelligence operatives who gave us *The Report From Iron Mountain* even proposed a powerful government agency or institution be set up to plan and carry out popularly accepted, new forms of ritualized Blood Games:

> An institution combining this function (blood games) with the preceding one (sophisticated, modern forms of human slavery), based on, but not necessarily imitative of, the precedent of organized ethnic repression, warrants careful consideration.

Real Life Blood Games

The United States has recently conducted a series of popular, real-life Blood Games—each of which was watched by the cheering, bloodlusty masses who observed the Games on big-screen televisions from the comfort of their living and family rooms. First, there were the smart bombs and missiles rained down on the Third World nation of Iraq. Our destruction of Iraqi forces was delivered with deafening blows by American military "gladiators" from the relative safety of high tech tanks, armored vehicles, jet aircraft, and computer-run ships.

Next on the Blood Game schedule was the U.S. initiated aggression against the Serb nation in Bosnia/ Yugoslavia. Americans and Europeans saw on television the visual feast of U.S. air strikes raining fire and death down on civilian skyscrapers, passenger trains, once tranquil neighborhoods, even fleeing flocks of refugees. We massacred tens of thousands supposedly to get at one man, a Mr. Slobodan Milosevic, who happened to be this poor nation's sitting political leader at the time. A Roman Emperor Commodus for a new era—that's what Milosevic was.

Sadam Hussein, Osama Bin Laden—each has been portrayed as a type of Commodus, worthy of death—but first, the Blood Games must be conducted. Call forth the American Gladiators!

He whom the elite rulers have chosen to be sacrificed must first be smeared and demonized. Randy Weaver?—he and his family were branded by the media as "white separatists." So—away with them. Off with their heads. Call in the gladiators!

David Koresh and his peaceful, if confused, congregation? "Cultists...weapons possessors." Oh my!—Kill them! Bring in the heavy artillery! Let the gladiators do their bloodwork!

Death and Blood Games as Entertainment

What we are seeing in the U.S.A., then, is a fascinating, if gruesome, updated reenactment of the ancient Blood Games of Rome but with a new, internet and television age, high tech slice of favor. In ancient Rome, criminals (in Rome, Christians were seen as dangerous "criminals") were executed and their executions became a vehicle for mass public entertainment. Now, American audiences are clamoring to watch on television convicts be put to death by lethal injection, by firing squad, and by electric chair. Better yet, public bloodlust demands that entire classes and groups of designated public enemies—even rogue nations!—be killed, with the wired public viewing the action live, staged as huge entertainment.

It was only natural that public lasciviousness progress in its debauchery from movie dramas like the *Texas Chainsaw Massacre* and *Scream* to greater, more jaw dropping realism. Even thrills and chills television shows like the reality-based *Survivor*, *Fear Factor*, *Spy TV*, *Jackass*, *Cops*, and others soon lose their ability to titillate. The desensitized masses will always want more and more. Shock value is fleeting. Bloodlust never diminishing.

Returning to *Gladiator*, my friend, Allen Woodham, director of South East Christian Witness, in Australia, observes:

> I have read reviews of the new blockbuster movie recently released called *Gladiator*. The fact that so many are going to see it proves that the same perverted bloodlust now exists in people that was present in the early Romans. Soon, they will grow weary of high tech "special effects" and demand something more "in your face" to obtain the same thrill...
>
> The deranged butchery of those early Roman days (when Christians were persecuted) should cause everyone to see where worldly entertainment is truly headed... The day could soon arrive when people will be in the bleachers watching Christians die.
>
> That might appear to be an over-reactionary statement to some. If you think this, it is only solid proof that your mind has already been satanically brainwashed by

Hollywood. (*South East Christian Witness*, April-May 2000, p. 14).

The Designated Enemy

The Holy Bible says that near the end of time, one, very special group shall be cast as the designated enemy—as the villains of society, as a collection of dangerous misfits. The Bible-believer who refuses to compromise his or her faith, who clings to Jesus, who says *no* to false Bible versions, *no* to homosexual perversion, *no* to murder of little babies through abortion, *no* to other gods and other religions—he or she shall become the publicly despised sacrifice of the prophesied Blood Games of *Revelation*.

Jesus said, "That whosoever killeth you will think that he doeth God service" *(John 16:2)*.

This, then, is how we as Christians should view the current mania for bloodlust. This is how we must understand and interpret the flood of fiendishness so prevalent in today's popular culture. The devil is now preparing and training the final generation of killers, desensitized and unfeeling, modern-day gladiators. The ultimate Blood Games are about to begin. The lions are hungry and in their cages. The new Emperor is about to take his throne and will oversee the bloodletting. Let the Games begin!

Even so, come quickly, Lord Jesus!

> — Texe Marrs, President
> *Power of Prophecy* Ministries
> Austin, Texas

FOREWORD

When Jesus sat upon the Mount of Olives, the disciples came unto him *privately*, saying, "Tell us, when shall these things be? And what shall be the sign of thy coming, and the end of the world?" (Matthew 24:3). Jesus immediately answered, "Take heed that no man deceive you." He continued, "For there shall arise false Christs, and false prophets, and shall shew great signs and wonders; insomuch that, if it were possible, they shall deceive the very elect." (Matthew 24:4-24).

Jesus warned his followers to be watchful and vigilant. The deception he spoke about was not going to be easily understood. It was going to be very subtle—so subtle, it would deceive even very well informed Christian men and women if it were possible.

Hopefully, this book may go some way toward unmasking that deception—a deception that finally culminates in the hands of one single man—a world ruler the bible prophetically calls antichrist.

This controversial book is written with a great deal of reticence and hesitancy. On the one hand, the author feels Christians should be properly informed. On the other hand, there is a clear biblical warning against resisting the power of world leaders or speaking evil of them.

"Let every soul be subject unto the higher powers. For there is no power but of God: *The powers that be are ordained of God.* Whosoever therefore resisteth the power, resisteth the ordinance of God: and they that resist shall receive to themselves damnation" (Romans 13:1-2).

Before reading this book, it is important to remember that God is still in complete control of world affairs. Sometimes this is difficult to understand. Pharaoh, Goliath, Nebuchadnezzar, Caesar, Nero, Titus, Diocletian, Charlemagne, Hitler and a host of others, all find their names in Romans 13:1-2, where their powers are all *ordained* of God. Christians need to be informed, but must also be mindful of Paul's warning in Romans. It is a sin to be ignorant (Numbers 15:22-31).

Saul was one of the most perfect 'types' of antichrist in scripture, yet he was the Lord's *anointed.* Having rejected God as their real king, Israel desired an earthly king like the pagan nations surrounding them, so God gave them Saul (I Samuel 8:7, 15:1). But the Lord's choice was David. Even while Saul was still alive, the Lord instructed Samuel to anoint David king. (I Samuel 16:13) In other words, there were two kings anointed in Israel at the same time. One was the 'people's choice,' the other was the 'Lord's choice.'

Saul sought to kill David. When David had the opportunity to defend himself by killing Saul, he didn't.

Instead, he cut off the skirt of Saul's robe and said, "The LORD forbid that I should do this thing unto my *master*, the LORD'S *anointed*, to stretch forth mine hand against him, seeing he is the *anointed* of the LORD" (I Samuel 24:6). While David already knew that Saul had been rejected he still gave him his respect as the Lord's anointed. In the last days, the time in which we are now living heralding Christ's second coming, there are to be *two kings* of Israel. One is the 'people's choice'— antichrist, the deceiver, and the other is the Lord's choice—Jesus Christ, who shall reign victorious.

In 2 Thessalonians chapter two, we are told that the man of sin, the Wicked One, whose coming is after the working of Satan with all power and signs and lying wonders, with all deceivableness of unrighteousness, is coming upon the world because "*they received not the truth, that they might be saved.*"

"*And for this cause* God shall send them strong *delusion*, that they should believe a lie: That they all might be damned who believeth not the truth, but had pleasure in unrighteousness."

Finally, like King Saul, a man is coming soon who is *appointed* by God to deceive every man, woman and child on earth who has rejected the truth. God himself is the author of this delusion which damns the unbeliever.

Like Israel of old, the apostate Church has now turned away from the truth and rejected the Lord. Great judgement is coming. The Lord is soon to give the 'Church' an earthly king 'of her choice' from within her ranks. One of his names is antichrist, and he is to become the New World Order leader. His opposite, of course, is the real King of Kings, Jesus Christ.

It is true this book casts world leaders in a negative

light. When the apostle Paul criticized the high priest, Ananias, the people who stood by, said, "Revilest thou God's high priest?" Paul immediately responded, "I wist not, brethren, that he was the high priest: for it is written, thou shalt not speak evil of the ruler of thy people." (Acts 23:1-5)

With this Godly admonition forever in mind, the reader is judiciously encouraged to read this book.

CHAPTER ONE

THE MOVIE: GLADIATOR
A Hero for the Ages

The movie *Gladiator* is being called "a great new classic, a retelling of ancient heroism packaged for today's minds." Winner of coveted awards and "Oscars," the movie's starring actor, Russell Crowe also has won high acclaim. What is this movie all about? Is it a story of the past—or is it, instead, a prophetically powerful cinema about our future?

It is 180 A.D; Emperor Marcus Aurelius and his Roman legions are involved in a bloody battle with the German barbarians in a fire-blackened forest north of Rome. The superior Roman troops survive triumphantly, killing most of the barbarians. Maximus, the heroic Roman general fights valiantly and is highly regarded by Marcus Aurelius. He is so impressed with Maximus's valour and leadership he exhibited in the battle that he promises the general his throne, instead of his very own son. Commodus is furious. Secretly he suffocates his elderly father and takes the throne before the emperor has time to give it to Maximus.

Upon taking power, the young Commodus sets about planning the murder of Maximus and his wife and son who are still living at home on the farm in Italy. The Roman soldiers murder his wife and son, but Maximus narrowly escapes. He goes into exile, is captured, becomes a slave, and finally is sold to a gladiator trainer in North Africa who brings him to Rome to be a star attraction at the Colosseum.

The self-conceited and evil Commodus effectively takes over as dictator. He is a despicable character. He attempts to have incestuous sexual relations with his glamorous sister Lucilla. If this is not enough, he craftily hints through subtle innuendo and gestures, he has paedophile desires for her son. He is a flaming sexual pervert, totally engrossed in himself and his own selfishness and importance. He shows no concern for others.

The corrupt, weak and gutless Senate follows Commodus's ruthless rule. He has a devious plan to use the gladiatorial games of the Colosseum for his own evil objectives. His purpose is to distract the masses' attention away from his own weakness, and divert their thoughts away from the impending doom facing the Roman Republic. The common people of Rome are partially deceived and subjugate themselves to evil Commodus, but deep down he has not gained their respect as a leader.

In the Colosseum arena, Maximus proves himself a mighty hero and valiant gladiator. Commodus is curious about the gladiator's identity and commands him to remove his helmet. The gladiator complies, and the emperor is shocked to discover it is none other than General Maximus who he thought he had murdered.

Fearing the reaction of the spectators, yet still wanting to kill Maximus, the emperor orders Maximus removed from the public arena. He then stabs Maximus with his dagger to weaken him before publicly fighting him in a duel in the arena. A terrible fight ensues and Maximus courageously succeeds in killing Commodus with the emperor's own dagger.

Deep down in their hearts, the crowds hate Commodus but love Maximus. Maximus briefly becomes the new emperor. Standing mortally wounded in the centre of the arena, not by the vote of the Senate, nor by the power of hereditary title, but only by the unanimous acclamation and the will of the people does he become emperor. For such a short time, he is the real hero, saviour and undisputed champion of the Roman people.

Mortally wounded, he dies on the sand of the Colosseum arena. Like Jesus Christ, he sacrifices himself for his people.

CHAPTER TWO

WHAT REALLY HAPPENED IN HISTORY?

Marcus Aurelius ruled the Roman Empire between 161—180 A.D. He proved himself one of the most industrious and certainly the most conscientious of the Roman emperors. He reverted to the old hereditary principle by passing the imperial succession on to his own son, Commodus. Apart from the fact they both persecuted Christians, the character and tastes of Commodus were the exact opposite of that of his philosophic father.

When Marcus Aurelius died, his son Commodus inherited the empire. A more worthless tyrant could not have sat on the imperial throne. He had a throne erected in the midst of the Senate. Clothed in a lion's skin, and holding a great club in his hand, he commanded the senators to offer sacrifice to him as if he were Hercules, the son of Jupiter.

He issued a decree summoning a general assembly

of the Senate in the Temple of the Earth adjacent to the Colosseum—all were to be present under pain of death. They imagined that some terrible calamity or emergency was threatening the empire. His decree was urgent.

One by one the senators entered. Seeing the emperor clothed in a lion's skin, some were immediately struck with fear and amazement, others were seized with laughter, as if the whole thing were a joke, for which they afterwards paid dearly. In consternation, others turned pale, for armed lictors were menacingly scattered throughout the temple.

The proud wretch Commodus addressed the senators; he declared that he had called them together for the purpose of announcing that henceforward he was to be worshipped as the son of Jupiter. No historian has left us an account of the derisory words he used. Who would chronicle such nonsense and impiety? But the Senate, the weak, fallen Senate, went through the blasphemous farce of incense and adulation worshipping him as a god. The cowardly Senate would rather worship the proud and lascivious Commodus, than to expose themselves to danger. Alas, this was true, but for one Christian senator. Not Maximus—but a man called *JULIUS.*

Over seven hundred aged senators tolerated the treacherous mockery—only Julius alone had the courage to express contempt and refuse to bend his knee. "How have you become so mad," asked Commodus, "as not to sacrifice to Jupiter and his son Hercules?" (We quote from the acts given by the Bollandists) Julius seemed for a moment too indignant to answer, but looking with contempt at the proud tyrant said, "You will perish like them because you lie like them." This was more than enough. The tyrant replied, "And who will save you and make us perish?"

Raising his finger solemnly toward heaven Julius said, "Jesus Christ." After a moment's pause, he added, "The one who condemns thee and thy foolish sovereign to eternal ruin."

The enraged Commodus ordered the guards to take him out to the Petra Scelerata to be scourged. While the brutal executioners were beating him, he died unexpectedly. Furious that the premature death of his honourable victim had left him unsatisfied, he ordered the blood-soaked body of Julius be cast before the statue of the sun, located near the arches of the Colosseum. He hoped the dogs might devour the body of the martyr and that the people pouring into the amphitheatre to see more Christians slaughtered, might see his infamy.

Guards were set to watch over his body, so that no one could remove it. A notice was put up on the walls of the Colosseum, announcing the death of Julius who was sacrificed for not worshipping the divinity of the great god who had just come amongst them, namely Commodus. Thousands of people pitied the fate of the brave man who had the courage to withstand the incredible absurdities of the cruel emperor.

The following night, when the guards were sound asleep, sympathetic Christians stole out from the arches of the Colosseum and took away the remains of the holy martyr, and buried them in the catacombs—where he lies to this very day together with his brethren, awaiting the resurrection of the saints.

Senator Julius, *not Maximus,* a <u>*true champion*</u> of the Roman Colosseum!

Like his father before him, only worse, Commodus was an intense persecutor of Christians. From the time of Augustus, the ordinary proceedings of the Senate commenced by sacrificing to Jupiter or Victory, whose statue was placed in their halls. Hence, as Baronius says (Anno 192), no senator could remain a member of the body after he had become a Christian; he was obliged to renounce the title or withdraw himself by voluntary exile.

Even from his youth, Commodus was a lewd, foul-mouthed and sadistic lad. He celebrated his adolescence by setting up a brothel of women with whom he disported himself. This was later to grow, when he became emperor, to a harem of three hundred women and three hundred boys, chosen expressly for their physical beauty and good looks. He indulged himself in the most decadent forms of sexual intercourse and sexual perversion. This often shocked even some of his most liberally-minded subjects. He often turned up at the Colosseum dressed as a woman, in which costume it pleased him to occupy the Imperial box.

According to Aubrey Menen's book, *Cities in the Sand*, pg.125, Commodus's sister was his first concubine.

It may be asked how such a man could rule the Empire. The simple answer is, he didn't! He left that to his favourites. The first was Perennis, but Commodus had him killed, along with his wife, his sister, and his two sons. The reason for this was a delegation from Britain had claimed Perennis was plotting to make his son emperor in Commodus' place. When Perennis died, Commodus appointed Cleander the favourite in his place. By this time, Commodus had almost totally collapsed Rome's finances and exhausted the Imperial treasure. Cleander set about raising money for the Emperor. Every office in the state was put up for sale, including that of the Consuls. He made twenty-four of them in one year.

The justice system was seriously corrupted under Commodus. While Cleander set about raising taxes to save the collapsing Imperial treasure, he introduced some desperate measures that affected the justice system. He created a policy where a rich criminal could not only buy his pardon; as an added touch, he could have the judge who condemned him together with the prosecution witnesses punished in turn, in a manner which could be of his own choosing.

The ordinary public took all this in its stride, until Cleander was so unwise as to let it touch the public's belly. He had a monopoly of the corn, which produced a famine. There was a riot. At length the crowd demanded the head of Cleander. Commodus tore himself away from his amusements long enough to order that Cleander's head be chopped off and given to the mob.

The parallels between the reign of Commodus and the time in which we live are incredible. Nations get the leaders they deserve. In another period, Roman citizens would never have put up with a leader like Commodus. Hypocrisy was the theme of this era. While privately expressing its disgust, the public and senators turned up and dutifully cheered their master—a man whom they all knew was willfully evil.

Commodus always made his entry into the Colosseum in great style. According to Dio Cassius, he wore a white silken tunic, interwoven with gold. He changed this for a purple robe with gold spangles and a crown made of gold, set with jewels from India. Since he considered himself Hercules, the symbols of that god— a lion's skin and a club—were carried before him, and solemnly given a chair to themselves in the Imperial box. He also had a fancy for being Mercury, so he carried Mercury's winged wand. When the time arrived for the games to begin, he made another change; he dressed in the simple dress of Mercury, a tunic and no sandals. Thus attired, the ruler of the world began the performance.

There is an excellent bust of Commodus in the Capitoline Museum. It is meant to be flattering, showing him as a handsome, well-built man, dressed as the re-incarnation of the god Hercules.

CHAPTER THREE

MAXIMUS, CONSTANTINE AND BRITAIN

In the film *Gladiator*, Commodus is accurately represented as being a tyrant lacking the love and respect of the people. Maximus, the real hero of the film, in reality is a fictitious character. Maximus in the movie, however, fulfils the role of a later leader in many respects—Constantine the Great.

Born in Britain in 272 A.D., Constantine became the great British leader of the Roman Empire. His mother was Welsh, daughter of Coelgodebog, Earl of Gloucester. In Britain she was called Ellen, but in Rome she was known as Helina. Constantine's father was a Roman, Caesar of the West, Constantius Chlorus. [*History of the Welsh Baptists* by J.Davis, page 10].

When Constantius died, Constantine was heroically proclaimed emperor, not by the Senate and leaders of Rome, but rather, by the will of the British people themselves and his army. The occasion took place at

York, July 25, 305 A.D. Constantine's mother, Helina, *greatly* helped Constantine to be so fondly loved and admired by the British and Roman people. She was a very pious woman and the most highly respected woman in the Roman Empire during her lifetime. She was the patron of many charitable works and had a reputation for helping people in need. (Very much like the British Queen Mother today).

Constantine was destined to become the great *ecumenical* 'prince' of the Roman people. Although he abolished the persecution of Christians and did much for the Church (with hindsight the persecutions of Diocletian may have been better), he still appealed to pagan and Christian subjects alike. It is doubtful if he really became a genuine Christian. However, when he knew he was dying, he was baptized by Eusebius on his deathbed where he passed away on May 22, 337 A.D.

In many ways, Constantine's reign as emperor fulfilled the role of a type of antichrist, because he synthesized Christianity and paganism under the cloak of the Roman State. Not long after he had died, Theodosius (378-395 A.D.) made church membership compulsory. This was the worst calamity that has ever befallen the Church. Christ had preached to conquer by purely voluntary means—the result of a genuine change of heart—not by force. The churches quickly became full of pagan and unregenerate people, and grew into a dragon from hell— the unholy Roman Catholic Church.

Constantine claimed to be a Christian, yet in his actions he was a defender of all faiths, not just the Christian faith. Like Israel of old, "they did that which was right in the sight of the LORD, but the high places were not taken away" (2 Chronicles 20:32-33). In May,

325 A.D., Constantine formally opened the First Ecumenical Council in Nicaea. Shortly afterwards, in the very next year, he put to death his son Crispus and his wife Fausta. (Hardly the actions of a real Christian). In many ways his actions have parallels with a certain, yet more recent ruler of Britain. (Events surrounding Lady Diana's demise were similar to Fausta's).

Britain, and especially Wales, have made a huge contribution to the growth of the Church. More so than any other Gentile nation on earth. The King James Bible did not just appear by chance in Britain. Its origin goes right back to the very beginning of the growth of the Church. Lucius, the Welsh king, was baptized the first king in the world to become a Christian. John Wycliffe (1324-384 A.D.) of England, the 'morning star' of the Reformation, translated the Bible into English and paved the way for the Reformation. William Tyndale, the translator of most of the text in the King James Bible New Testament, was born near the border between England and Wales. His parents were members of the Baptist Church at Abergaverney, South Wales. Out of the English Church came the Puritans, Baptists, Methodists, etc. who colonized America and gave the New World her freedom that broke the yoke of Rome. Britain's role in spreading Christianity is profound.

It is important to remember that Diocletian's terrible persecutions lasted over ten years throughout the rest of the Roman Empire, but less than one year in Britain. Under Diocletian, the Caesar of the West, Constantius Chlorus (Constantine's father) wouldn't put anyone to death in Britain, unlike the rest of the Roman Empire that was drenched in blood. The reason for this was that many people in Britain had become Christians, including even members of Constantius's own household and Roman officials. They simply wouldn't implement Diocletian's deadly edicts. By 305 A.D., over one half of the entire population of Britain were Christians.

For the British people to have turned away from 'the great Faith' of their early Christian forefathers, as they now have, is simply an *'ABOMINATION.'* If ever Daniel's apocalyptic warning about antichrist "...*Neither shall he regard the God of his fathers...* " (Dan. 11:36-37) has any prophetic application, it applies to the British Heir and Sovereign!

As the whole world now apostatizes in chaos and rebellion, could it be a modern Constantine the Great, a Prince from Wales, a Monarch from London (London & Wales—whose Coats of Arms are both red dragons), and a Royal Family who claim to be heirs of the Lion of Judah, ruling on the throne of David—could it be he, who is really the one who is cast as <u>Maximus</u> in the film *GLADIATOR?*

Not as the corrupt Commodus—a paedophile—who by hereditary possession and murder gained his title as Emperor. But as hero and champion of the Middle East Arena is he worshipped ("arena" in Latin means "sand"). Surrounded by peoples of every nation on earth, the spectators in the giant, New World Order Roman Colosseum, a counterfeit prince of peace and saviour of the world. Crowned not by the Senate, but by the will of the people—the master *Gladiator* of the Roman Colosseum!

CHAPTER FOUR

IN PRAISE OF THE WORLD HERO: NAZI PROPAGANDA AND MODERN DECEPTION

How one single person could deceive a civilized nation like Germany is almost beyond our comprehension. Only now—in retrospect—do we now know it was the result of one single man—Propaganda Minister Joseph Goebbels!

From the beginning to the end, the minds of the ordinary citizenry of the Third Reich were controlled by this one man. During his diabolical ministry he ordered that all Nazi *films* concentrate not on information and fact, but on emotion and entertainment. He brought his passion of Hollywood epics like *Gone with the Wind* to the making of Nazi films and newsreels.

Film techniques were cunningly used to portray the Fuhrer as a man apart, a father and god-like figure who possessed super-human abilities and sacrificed himself for his nation. Like a masterful Hollywood producer, Goebbels was careful not to over-expose his favourite star but preferred the Fuhrer to appear in short newsreels only. A whole 'sequel' of films were subtly created and released *over a number of years* and used to deceive the German people en masse.

Streams and streams of '*HISTORICAL films*' were made up to portray great German personalities such as Frederick the Great, Bismarck and Schiller, that made a parallel of the past with the present. Without mentioning Hitler's name, the films subtly captured the people's imagination that there was a similar situation in the past compared to the present one. All these films had one great theme. They implicitly compared the Fuhrer with the heroes of the past. Goebbels preferred pictures to speak for themselves, with the script only filling in the message with what the audience would not otherwise understand.

In 1940, Hitler ordered film propaganda warfare against the Jews. Heinrich Himmler, Commander of the SS, instructed all those under his command to view the anti-Jewish film *Jud Sub* (Jew Suss) released in 1940. The film was a huge success. Nazi audience research showed that almost all of the audience had made the connection between the events of 18th century Wurttemberg portrayed in the film—and 20th century Germany.

A 1941 film, *Soldaten von Morgen* (Soldiers of Tomorrow), portrayed any future leader of England as a '*son*' of Britain with a cigar in his mouth looking like the '*father*' of Britain, Winston Churchill. The script read: "The whole world knows that the '*son*' will be like the '*father*'."

In the film *Gladiator,* this phrase is deftly used through subtle innuendo in the characters of Marcus Aurelius *(father)* and his evil *(son)* Commodus, to draw a parallel with **George Bush (Snr)** *(father)* and **George Bush (Jnr)** *(son)*.

Because the character roles in *Gladiator* are so blatant and glaring, **it seemed plain in advance that George Bush (Jnr) *('son')* would be elected the President of the United States of America.** The script-writers of *Gladiator* **already knew** the corrupt background of the N.W.O. Bush family. *George Bush (Jnr) had 'ALREADY BEEN CHOSEN' as the new President!*

In the film *Gladiator,* released in the year 2000, Commodus's sister is called **'Lucilla.'** (The name of a famous 3rd century Roman Christian martyr). In propaganda terms, the name 'Lucilla' has a close psychological resemblance to 'Laura,' the wife of the coming new President of the United States:—**George / 'Commodus' Bush (Jnr)!**

Even as late as 1945, at the end of the war, Goebbels concentrated on one last film which proved to be his greatest legacy. *Kolberg* was a *'HISTORICAL'* drama about the heroic resistance the Germans of Kolberg had valiantly put up against Napoleon's army. Goebbels was so obsessed with this film that he diverted over 100,000 soldiers from the front-line and made them act in it as extras. (Now Hollywood does this by computer.)

The people of Germany were so deceived that even at the end of the war, when their towns were burning, the vast majority of the population were *still* queuing up in the streets to watch these seductive films!

Surely a terrible indictment against the public masses—a tribute to the skill of the Nazi Propaganda

Minister—a final warning to the entire world.

If a man such as Goebbels could manipulate the mind of a cultured nation like Germany like a primitive children's puppet, surely one day—without proper guidance and vigilance, such a man would inevitably do it to the whole world.

Modern history has shown that not only in Goebbel's Germany, but in Lenin's Russia, Mao's China, Castro's Cuba, Pol Pot's Cambodia, and Clinton's U.S.A., similiar propaganda tactics have proven temendously effective.

Revelation 12:9 warns about a great red dragon, Satan, going forth to *'deceive' the <u>whole</u> world.* The events in Germany during World War II were a final warning for what soon is to come.

CHAPTER FIVE

NEW WORLD ORDER: GLADIATOR PROPAGANDA

The years since the end of the Second World War have seen the greatest advances in technology the world has ever seen. Hitler only dreamed about the powers of the modern Hollywood director. The present-day New World Order Psychological Warfare 'Propaganda Minister,' having studied Goebbels manipulative techniques to the letter and aided by modern technological advances, is thousands of times more subtle, more persuasive, more crafty, more cunning, more clever than ever Hitler looked like being!

The most advanced mind control in films deploys high-level "witchcraft." Virtually all American witchcraft comes from England. In Britain the old-world Druid priests had magical wands made out of *'Holly-wood'*—hence the name 'Hollywood'. Modern-day *'Holly-wood'* directors are simply modern-day Druid priests specializing in 'high witchcraft,' directed not from America, but from London and the Vatican. The Vatican sits on one of the seven hills of Rome and the former site of the Temple of Aesculapius in the city. Aesculapius was worshipped as a man and a serpent. Sometimes he was worshipped as half-man and half-serpent. He is often shown as a serpent wrapped around a tree, which symbolized the new-born god Baal-berith, *'Lord of the Covenant.'* (He is the infamous character alluded to in Daniel 9:27 who "shall confirm the [Jerusalem?] *covenant* with many for one week.")

'Vatican' is derived from the Latin word *'vaticinator'* meaning *'prophet.'* In Revelation 16:13, John "saw three unclean spirits like *frogs* come out of the mouth of the *dragon*, and out of the mouth of the beast, and out of the mouth of the *false prophet.*" The mouth of the London dragon and the mouth of the Roman hypnotizing snake of the false prophet have a big input in world events in the last days centred on Jerusalem and the Middle East.

Following Goebbels past examples, a whole stream of propaganda films are now being shown in movie theatres and on television. They are being carefully launched with one sole purpose in mind—to <u>mesmerize</u> the whole world into accepting a New World Order. This is a New World Government (Beast) based upon the old Roman system of dictatorship where ultimately the supreme leader's powers are absolute and he is not responsible to the Senate. The level of perfection, achieved in modern productions, makes Goebbel's films look like amateurish rejects. Film propaganda and subliminal persuasion is now a highly developed science. The films with the strongest message, and most deceptive, are the ones we least expect. *Gladiator* is only the beginning.

Good examples of others are *The Lion King,*
Pocahontas and *Prince of Egypt.* These films are all
about an *ecumenical prince,* a *lion,* a *saviour* and a
peacemaker. Each individual film is but a short sequel,
a chapter in the complete book. With each sequel comes
a new revelation.

In *The Lion King,* Scar is the evil leader who throws
the world into chaos. In *Prince of Egypt* he is Pharaoh.
In *Pocahontas* he is 'Governor Radcliff. In *Gladiator*
he is Emperor Commodus. During the reign of these
evil leaders there is war and famine. During this time of
chaos, the true heir to the throne or people's champion,
hero and saviour goes into <u>exile</u>. Only when the chaos
is at its worst, when there appears to be no redemption,
is the evil leader challenged by the true heir. Just when
there appears to be *'no hope,'* the hero defeats him, and
becomes fully recognized for who he really is—the
champion and saviour of the world.

In *The Lion King,* the true heir to the throne of the
animal world is Simba. At the beginning of the film,
evil Scar murders Simba's father and usurps the throne
ahead of young Simba. The Prince Simba goes into exile,
during which time evil Scar turns the animal world into
chaos and starvation. Finally, when there is no food,
Rafiki the baboon prophet (representing the leader of
the World Church) leads Simba back to defeat Scar,
bringing peace to the world. Rafiki finally crowns the
'prince of peace,' Simba, the Lion King on a giant jutting
rock ledge, from where he rules. This ledge in the film
is an almost exact representation of the jutting rock
ledge in Pergamos where the temple of Zeus and
Pergamon altar were located 800 feet high up a mountain.
[Presently, as at July 2000, the *Pergamon altar* resides

in the Pergamon Museum, Berlin, Germany.] This is the altar referred to in Revelation 2:12-13 which reveals where Satan's seat is. This may be the location of the seat of power of the New World Leader (provided the altar continues to reside there).

It is important to remember that at the time John wrote the book of Revelation, the people worshipped Caesar at Pergamos even more than did the people living in Rome. (Pergamos was Caesar's second home, but he did not live there permanently). Simba, the *Lion King* is a counterfeit of Jesus Christ, the real *Lion* of Judah, Prince of Peace and King of Kings.

The animated film *Pocahontas* is the sequel following *Lion King*. In 1607, King James of England bids farewell to Governor Radcliff and his men who depart on a ship sailing for the New World in America. While crossing the Atlantic a man is washed overboard in a storm. Captain John Smith dives overboard and courageously saves him. Immediately, he gains the respect of his men. Deep down, they have more respect for John Smith than for the Governor—(Americans may wish to speculate exactly which particular *'Governor'* Radcliff represents). ('John Smith' is also a pseudonym for a man with 'No Name.' In high-level Luciferian witchcraft, there is a principality called 'No Name'—sometimes he is called the 'Nameless One.' He is the 'Nameless One' in the Harry Potter books identified as 'Voldemort'—which in French means 'flight of death')

Upon arriving in the New World, Governor Radcliff tries to steal the gold off the American Indians and kill them. (the Indians represent "all" Americans). During this period John Smith meets Pocahontas and is betrothed to her. (Hitler believed the whole German nation was his bride.) Antichrist's bride will be an unbelieving world. At the conclusion of the film, our hero John Smith from England saves the American Indians from evil Governor Radcliff. (Alias Governor Clinton, Governor George Bush (Jnr).) Standing on a 'Lion-King Rock,' Pocahontas affectionately bids her sweetheart farewell, waving goodbye, as the champion of both the American Indians and his own men departs on a ship back to England.

The *'Lion King'* in this sequel thus becomes the 'saviour of the New World' from England. Gradually the plot thickens.

In the next dizzying sequel, *'The Prince of Egypt'* — contrary to the true biblical account of Moses, who worshipped *only* the God of Israel—the film portrays Moses as a *'Lion King'* arch-type. An ecumenical character who appeals both to the Egyptians as well as to the Hebrews.

Steven Spielberg openly claims the film is not a true biblical story, but is deliberately crafted to appeal not to just one faith, but all faiths.

The film is universal, dubbed into twenty-eight languages and is aimed at adults as well as children. When Spielberg's London-based company folded, one hundred and twenty English animators flew to Los Angeles to work for Dreamworks SKG. In spring of 1998, the music for *The Prince of Egypt* was recorded in London. Spielberg often says the 'heroes' in films like *Lion King* and *Lawrence of Arabia* are all Moses-type figures. The theme is the same. Out of chaos, One World Leader!

In the film *Gladiator*, virtually all the cinema advertising includes a picture of Maximus, above which is the caption: *'A Hero will Rise.'* Strangely, the leading role of hero Maximus is played by a New Zealander, Russell Crowe.

New Zealand is a small, enchanting country of 3.9 million people located in the South Pacific off the eastern coast of Australia. A member of the British Commonwealth, the people speak with an 'ecumenical' English accent—neither Australian, nor Oxford English, nor American. Little New Zealand has long been a favourite daughter of the British Monarch. In propaganda terms she is neutral. New Zealanders fill a high proportion of world leadership roles, far out of proportion to the size and population of their little country. Dame Kiri Te Kanawa sang at Charles' and Diana's wedding. Don McKinnon is presently the British Commonwealth Secretary General. The late ex Prime Minister Sir Robert Muldoon was head of the International Monetary Fund. Mike Moore is presently the Director General of the World Trade Organization. (In July 2000, he also played a key role in the New York Integrated Framework Summit Meeting, involving six key international agencies which included the WTO, International Monetary Fund, the World Bank and the United Nations Conference on Trade and Development.) Peter Watson was Chairman of the United States International Trade Commission and spent two years working in the White House as trade lawyer on WTO issues.

Dr Kennedy Graham is Secretary General of Parliamentarians for Global Action (formerly, Parliamentarians for World Order) based in New York, and so on.

The psychological effect of having Crowe act the role of Maximus, the archetype of the coming antichrist world leader, was inevitable. With an accent that is neither

European nor American, nor coming from the world's leading two belligerent world powers, he stands aloof from religious and political differences—taking no side in the Senate's squabbles.

Nor is he driven by the desire for money or power, but only by his own courage and sacrifice does he become the hero. Totally neutral in every respect, exempt from the disdain of the weak and corrupt Senate.

Only by the unanimous consent of the Colosseum audience does he slay evil Commodus. Only by the will and resounding acclamation of the Roman people was he made emperor. Maximus becomes emperor, not by force, financial backing, corruption, nor even of his own volition—but by the sheer praise, worship, love and respect of the Roman people.

In every respect, almost, a substitute of Jesus Christ.

CHAPTER SIX

MAXIMUS: ST. GEORGE AND THE DRAGON

Maximus, originally a *farm worker* who became a valiant Roman soldier—who slew evil Commodus, then sacrificed himself for his people.

Saint George, whose name, George, literally means *'Earth Worker'*—who became a Roman centurion, a valiant Christian soldier—who slew the evil dragon, then sacrificed himself for his people.

Saint George—the patron saint of all England and founder of the Order of the Garter (the highest order of Freemasonry; the head of which is the British Sovereign)—revered in Russia and the Moslem world alike. The champion of religious liberty, the victorious one, the captain of the noble army of martyrs. The environmental 'Ever-green green one,' Prince of the Earth.

Saint George was born in 270 A.D. at Lydda, called Diospolis (city of Jove) by the Romans, and martyred at Nicomedia on April 23, 304 A.D. According to myth, he just happened to live to the age of thirty-three, the same age of Jesus Christ—who was martyred so that many might be saved. He served as a soldier in the army of the Roman Emperor Diocletian, the most wicked persecutor of Christians the world has ever seen. (A strange vocation, to say the least, for a Christian martyr!)

At the time the true followers of Christ were being persecuted for *not* serving in the Roman legions because Christ taught them to love their enemies—because part of the requirement of serving in the Roman army was to take an oath of allegiance to the emperor and to Jupiter. The emperor Diocletian had made Nicomedia (Ismidt) on the south shores of the Bosphorus, his eastern and principal capital, and his chief residence.

Eusebius, in his eighth Book of Ecclesiastical History, says that Anthimus, Bishop of Niomedia, was one of the *first* witnesses (martyrs) to be beheaded. On February 24, 303 A.D., Galerius and Diocletian were at Nicomedia and passed edicts against the Christians. This was the day after the demolition of the church.

According to the pagan legend, St. George valiantly appealed to Diocletian to spare his Christian brethren, and he was beheaded on April 23, 304 A.D., *over a year later*. If St. George really was such a valiant and *famous* Christian martyr as they claim, Eusebius would surely have included him by name with his history of prominent martyrs like Anthimus, Bishop of Nicomedia. The truth is he didn't do it.

Both the Russians and the United Nations love the mythical martyr. In October 1990, a bronze statue depicting St. George slaying the dragon (made of actual United States and Soviet missile parts) created by Zurab Tsaratali, was gifted by the Soviet Government to the

United Nations and installed in New York. The victorious saint, it seems, is not only the protector of Britain, but now, of Russia, the United States and the United Nations.

Every year, Saint George's Feast Day in the Church of England is observed on April 23—the **same day** as the Feast of **Vinalia,** the *greatest* ancient pagan feast day on the Roman calendar. The *Vinalia* was dedicated to the 'supreme god' of the Roman people—*Jupiter,* that, by the way, is the pagan counterfeit of the Old Testament Hebrew <u>*JEHOVAH.*</u>

The name of Jesus is derived from the Hebrew 'Joshua,' which literally means: <u>*'JEHOVAH SAVES.'*</u> Therefore, *Jupiter* and the *Vinalia* are also the pagan counterfeit of the <u>*LORD JESUS CHRIST.*</u> In Rome, the pagan sun-god was called Jupiter or Jove. In Greece, his sacred name was Zeus and there he was known as the 'Sin-bearer.' In India, he was known as the 'Victim-man.' Among the Buddhists of the East he was called the 'Saviour of the World.' The Greeks called him 'Zeus the Saviour.' In Egypt, he was named 'King of Kings' and 'Lord of Lords.' He was the 'Hero-god' and given a name above all names. Highly honoured, he was worshipped as the 'Great World King.'

Saint George's blood-red cross is on the flag of *Protestant* 'merrie' England. The sign of 'Victory' and the champion of 'Ecumenism.' The pagan sun-god of the apostate *Protestant* Church. Dressed in 'christianized' robes, 'saviour of the world,' Saint George—Emperor Maximus, the British sovereign!

Commodus, the weak and corrupt, Roman Emperor— the paedophile and leader of the gutless Senate. Son of an emperor who hated Christians. Commodus lost the respect of the Senate and the Roman people:

George Bush (Jnr), a limited, weak, and corrupt president. Son of a father who, also a president, lost the respect of the Senate and the American people. Who plunged the whole world into chaos, in the sands of the Middle East arena.

Maximus, the British Sovereign, yet **_no longer_** the British king. Saint George, surrounded by the crowds of the world Colosseum. The victorious gladiator, champion of religious liberty. Worshipped by Jew, Moslem and Christian alike. The coming *'Prince of Peace'* of the Middle East arena. **The World King!**

Born in the City of Jove (Jupiter). Died on the *Vinalia*. If ever there was a character who represented the arch-enemy of Jesus Christ, it would have to be an apostate Christian soldier who served in the army of Diocletian!

CHAPTER SEVEN

THE ROMAN COLOSSEUM

The release of the epic film *Gladiator*, coincided with the opening of the ancient Colosseum in Rome for spectacles and paying audiences. Surely this did not happen by chance. The opening ceremony conducted by Italian Culture Minister Giovanna Melandri, in July 2000, heralded once again a solemn warning for Jews and Christians. If history repeats itself, and it looks like it shall, a time of great persecution is coming for those who will not give their allegiance to Jupiter.

After 1500 years of dereliction, the infamous amphitheatre was innocently opened for various cultural festivals and performances. A costly stage has been built at the eastern end of the Colosseum near the podium where the emperor, his court and senators used to give the thumbs up or thumbs down to decide the gladiator's fate. And of course, to watch the Christians and enemies of the state being slaughtered. The stage is being set.

All around the world, in every nation, giant stadiums are being built just as they were in the Roman Empire.

Some are being brazenly named after the Roman Colosseum itself. In Rome, the spectacles started with sports events and entertainment, then quickly graduated to wild beast fights, then animals against humans, then humans against humans. Gladiators, slaves and Christians were the principal victims. Finally, no entertainment was popular unless accompanied by cruelty and bloodshed.

When Nero conceived the idea of satiating the rage of the people by the blood of the Christians, the smoking ruins of the burnt city were *still* smouldering. Lit under the orders of the emperor himself, the destructive **'fires' heralded an imminent 'state of emergency.'** No sooner were his terrible decrees promulgated throughout the empire, before the whole pagan world switched immediately, and became possessed with demons. Instantaneously, overnight, one's friends became one's enemies. Christians and Jews were treated the same— enemies of the state.

Emperor Augustus first conceived the erection of the great amphitheatre and Vespasian commenced its construction in 72 A.D. It took eight years to build and was dedicated by Titus in 80 A.D., though it was not completely finished until the reign of Domitian. More than thirty thousand workers were constantly employed in its construction. The workmen were captive Jews who were taken from Jerusalem after its desolation under the triumph of Titus. Jesus Christ was sold by the Jews for thirty pieces of silver; after the triumph of Titus, you could get thirty Jews for one piece of silver. (Today, the Church could do well to heed that.)

The designs of amphitheatres at Capua, Verona and Pompeii were similar to those of Rome. The complete ground plan of the Colosseum may be seen in the Minerva

Library, a few hundred yards from the old ruin itself. The horrors of the Colosseum were repeated in other stadiums of the Roman Empire.

It is important to remember the Colosseum was regarded as a *"temple" dedicated to Jupiter.* About two hundred yards from the amphitheatre stood a smaller temple which served for the ordinary rites and sacrifices. This temple was dedicated to the goddess of the Earth. The temple is said to have served from time to time for the assemblies of the Senate, and for the tribunal chair of a praetor. Being in the very heart of the ancient city and near the Colosseum, it was the spot where the Christians were most frequently taken and offered in sacrifice. Standing before this temple was a monument which witnessed the cruelest and bloodiest scenes of those terrible times. Its very name of *Accursed* or *Criminal Stone* (Petra Scelerata) tells of the indescribable horror in which it was held even by the Roman public themselves. It was a sort of elevated stage, on which there was an immense slab of marble where public malefactors and criminals were executed. It was here that many of the noblest Christians were martyred...

... and it was here, evil Commodus had the victorious Christian senator, **Julius** (*not Maximus)*, dragged naked in chains. Where he was flogged until death had released his spirit and his body was exposed to public gaze.

CHAPTER EIGHT

HOLOCAUST (APRIL 15-19)

Of special note for luke-warm Jews and Christians, who feel that *Gladiator* is _just another_ film—it may be worth considering that the Roman architect of the Colosseum was a Christian, Gaudentius—its *first martyr!* A stone slab which contains an inscription to him can be seen at present in the subterranean church of St. Martin in the Forum.

When Commodus called the senators together to offer sacrifice to himself as if he were Hercules the son of Jupiter, the General Assembly was held in the *Temple of the Earth.* Standing before this temple was the Petra Scelerata, the accursed stone. Each year on April 15th, the feast of *Fordicidia* was held in this temple, consecrated to Tellus, the Mother-Earth goddess. It involved sacrificing a pregnant cow to Tellus. During this important ceremony the unborn calf was burned whole.

This whole burnt offering was called the ***Holocaust***. Throughout pagan history the major burnings of Jews and Christians have occurred on or near this date. The

Roman pagan *Fordicidia* is the same feast as the Feast of Ishtar, consecrated to the mother-earth goddess 'Ishtar' of Babylon—that has since been 'christianized' and celebrated as 'Easter' by the apostate Christian Church. [In Babylon, Ishtar was symbolized by a lion—that is why Commodus clothed himself in a lion's skin in the Temple of the Earth.]

The four great Roman feasts are a counterfeit of Jewish *Passover and Seven Days of Unleavened Bread.* The Devil is very precise! The *Fordicidia* held on April 15th is the satanic substitute for Jewish Passover. (Christians believe Jesus Christ is the Passover Lamb of God.)

Immediately following the *Fordicidia* and celebrated in conjunction with this first sacred feast comes the *Cerialia.* This feast is consecrated to the cereal goddess Ceres, held on April 19th every year. Immediately following the *Cerialia* comes the *Parilia*, held on April 21st, consecrated to the goddess Pales who is the goddess of shepherds and their flocks. This day is <u>still</u> celebrated as the birthday of Rome. Lastly, comes the greatest feast of Rome, the *Vinalia,* consecrated to the supreme god Jupiter, the god of light (Lucifer)—the *sun*, the protector of vines and the Roman people. His feast has a special double articulation on the Roman calendar, April 23rd and August 19th.

Jupiter was also honoured on the *'ides'* of each month, which fell on the 13th of most months excepting March, May, July and October when they fell on the 15th. A *"lamb"* was sacrificed to Jupiter on these dates (a monthly reminder of Rome's *hate* of the Jewish Passover). The pagan Roman Catholic <u>**Fatima Apparitions**</u> in 1917 were synchronized to these particular dates, as was the planned (now failed) end of the 'Middle East Peace Accord' on Sept.13th, 2000.

Genuine Christians believe that Jesus Christ is the real *Passover* lamb of God, and not the *Fordicidia*. They believe that Jesus is the true *Unleavened Bread* of life of the world that came down from heaven, and not the *Cerialia*. They believe that Jesus Christ their LORD is the true good *Shepherd* of the sheep, and not the *Parilia*. And lastly, they believe that only Jesus Christ is the true *Light* of the world and the true *Vine*, their 'protector,' and certainly not Jupiter or the *Vinalia*.

Unlike Jewish Passover, the feast of great sacrifice, Jesus' death, which occurred in the late afternoon, the Roman Holocaust of the *Fordicidia* through to the *Cerialia* was held in the morning (dedicated to mother-earth and the rising sun). Jesus was **crucified** in the morning, this author believes, during the *Fordicidia/Cerialia* [Easter period], a year in which Easter and Passover coincided, but **_died_** on Passover in the late afternoon.

Much can be said how these ancient pagan 'nature' feasts dominate the pagan mind. During the Second World War Hitler changed *'May Day'* to the *Cerialia*. At **_precisely_** 9 a.m. in the morning of _Jewish Passover_, April 19th, 1943, the **_exact time_** that the *Cerialia* would have been sacrificed in ancient Rome, the Nazis commenced to burn the Jewish Warsaw ghetto to the ground. Using tanks with flame-throwers, *"a whole burnt offering of a pregnant cow,"* they proceeded forth to burn men, women and children. Again, at 9 a.m., in the morning of April 19th, 1993, amazingly, **_exactly_** fifty years later to the day—the Waco, Texas, Branch Davidian Complex was burnt to the ground—using tanks and flame-throwers—burning men, women and children. This time, not by an evil Nazi world leader, but ordered by the President and Attorney General of the United States. That very evening, President Clinton had the arrogance and effrontery to open the *Holocaust* Memorial Museum in Washington, D.C.

More recently, at precisely 9 a.m. in the morning of April 19, 1995, the federal building in Oklahoma City exploded and crashed to the ground. "America's Kids Day Care Centre" was located in one of the lower floors. I believe the attack was ordered by a President who lied and said: "The bombing in Oklahoma City was an attack by false patriots on innocent children."

Will the United States now go on to re-enact Nero's *burning* of Rome, or Hitler's *burning* of the old Nazi Reichstag Building? Are the Waco and Oklahoma *Cerialia sacrifices* a symptom of a much deeper pervading evil in the American government administration? The facts certainly indicate this is so.

On March 24, 1997, John Newbury, Press and Information officer for the World Council of Churches Office of Communication in Geneva issued an important press release stating:

"*THE DATE OF EASTER: SCIENCE OFFERS SOLUTION TO ANCIENT RELIGIOUS PROBLEM:* Senior church representatives have come up with an ingenious proposal to set a common date for Easter. At present, churches in the East and West celebrate Easter, the Resurrection of Jesus Christ from the dead, on two different dates in most years—Differences in dating occur because churches follow different calculations of the equinox and the full moon—It is suggested that the new method of calculation begin in *2001*, when the date of Easter, using the old methods and the new, will be the same, viz. *April 15ᵗʰ*, and that a common date be kept from then on."

Thus, from <u>APRIL 15, 2001</u>, the apostate World Church will wickedly celebrate the pagan Roman "<u>FORDICIDIA</u>." Will this herald the start of the coming New World Order "<u>HOLOCAUST?</u>" Will this have something to do with evil Commodus in *Gladiator*? Who sacrificed the valiant Christians and burnt them in the fires consecrated to Tellus in the Temple of the Earth— cruelly murdered like the courageous souls in the Colosseum arena.

ALL of the pagan religions in the world have one thing in common:—they worship the *sun—[fire-god] and mother-earth*. The names they give him and her may be different, but they are the *same* deities. When Israel apostatized, she rejected JEHOVAH and worshipped the Babylonian *sun-god* and *mother-earth*. For her sin and rebellion, she finally was *burnt with fire*.

At the beginning of the year 2000, the major 'new millennium' ceremony of the world was held in the *Millennium Dome* in London. There, the whole ceremony was conducted over a raised, witchcraft, hexagram high altar in the centre of the stage. The central part of the satanic ritual consecrated a bright-green laser emerald (representing *Hermes*—the Babylonian *sun-god*) as the new 'prince' and 'leader' of the New World Order. With a representation of the Pergamon Altar on the wall of the Dome at the back of the stage, the light of the dawning new-age sun was visible through a large wrought-iron "arch" representing the *earth-mother* goddess's womb.

Surrounded by *fire*-works and incense, and a burning brazier to Baal on the Thames, dressed in bright-red, with the accompaniment of two children singing a hymn to lord-Lucifer, the high-priestess of world witchcraft, the Defender of the Faith of the Protestant Church, Queen Elizabeth II, the royal patron, presided over the satanic ritual.

As the Protestant Church now apostatizes and rejects Jesus Christ as her Creator, she, too, is turning back and joining Rome. A Roman Catholic Church that has for centuries joined with all the pagan religions of the world in worshipping '*nature*,' the Babylonian *sun-god* and his *mother-earth* goddess, *Ishtar*, now becomes the Protestant's partner. Finally, there arises a great "World Church of the Goddess of the Earth." For her sin and rebellion, she, too, like ancient Jerusalem and Babylon, is soon to be ***burnt with fire.*** (Revelation 18:8).

CHAPTER NINE

HERO: PONTIFEX MAXIMUS

The Roman Emperor Diocletian has long been recognized by the Church as the greatest persecutor of Christians the world has ever seen. It just so happens that the name of 'Maximus,' the 'hero' in the film Gladiator, was a title Diocletian personally applied to Himself!

In the Vatican Museum in Rome, there is an infamous stone slab upon which is the solemn inscription:

"DIOCLETIANUS IOVIUS ET MAXIMIANUS
HERCULES CAES. AUG.
AMPLIFICATO PER. ORIENTEM ET
OCCIDENTEM IMP. ROM.
ET
NOMINE CHRISTIANORUM
DELETO, QUI REMP. EVER-
TEBANT."

["Diocletian Jupiter and Maximianus (*MAXIMUS*) Hercules, Caesars, having extended the Roman Empire through the East and West, and destroying the name of the Christians who were ruining the state."]

One would have to be blind to believe *"Maximus"* was just an innocent, randomly chosen name in the film. The fact is: his name was deeply researched and carefully chosen.

It is sobering to reflect upon Diocletian's edict of hate and suffering. It is gratifying to remember he failed miserably. His inscription was a lie, for he never was able to completely destroy the faith of the Christians. It is an indisputable fact, that more Romans than ever became Christ's followers because of the emperor's persecutions. [Unlike the reign of Constantine].

The scriptwriters of the film *Gladiator,* the modern successors of Diocletian, had good reason to name their hero 'Maximus.'

Originally, the term 'Sovereign Pontiff' or 'Pontifex Maximus' applied to Nimrod, the first pagan king of Babylon. The title continued to be used by the kings of Babylon until the empire came to an end. On the death of Bel-shaz-zar, and the expulsion of the Chaldean priesthood from Babylon by the Medo-Persian kings, the seat (or throne) of power was taken to Pergamos. In Babylon, the supreme pagan deity, the *'sun,' incarnated in the King*, was worshipped as 'a man,' and was worshipped as the image of 'a man.' In Pergamos, the deity Aesculapius was represented as 'a man' who was incarnated in the king.

Pergamos became an integral part of the Roman Empire when Attalus III, the last of its kings, at his death, left by will all his dominions to the people of Rome, in 133 B.C.

When Julius Caesar, who had previously been elected

'Pontifex (Pope) Maximus,' became emperor and head of the Roman state and religion, all powers and functions of the legitimate Babylonian Pontiff were vested in him. On certain occasions, while carrying out his high pontifical office, he appeared in the pomp of the Babylonian costume inherited from Attalus; just as Bel-shaz-zar himself might have done, in robes of scarlet, with the crozier of Nimrod in his hand, wearing the mitre of Dagon and bearing the keys of Janus and Cybele.

This custom was religiously perpetuated by the Roman emperors until the reign of Gratianus (Gratian) who ruled 375—383 A.D. Gratian was the first emperor who refused to appear in the idolatrous pontifical attire, and to act as Pontifex. Ironically, in 383 A.D., while endeavouring to combat the usurper 'Maximus,' he was captured at Lyons in France and there put to death.

No sooner was the old paganism of the Roman state legally abolished before it was insidiously revived by the very emperor who had abolished it. Subsequently it was bestowed upon the Bishop of the Roman Church. Thus, the Bishop of Rome became the Sovereign Pontiff— the Pope of Rome, *Pontifex Maximus—'a man'* from Babylon who reigned over the Dark Ages of the Roman Catholic Church. (The literal meaning of *'Pontifex Maximus'* is 'chief bridge builder'.)

Finally, the yoke of Rome was broken by the Reformation and the Protestant Church. No longer was the Roman Sovereign the supreme Pontiff Maximus. No longer was he the grand 'Papa,' the reincarnated sun-god ruling over his mother-earth goddess, Europa, the entire earth.

In 1611, the British Sovereign, King James I, head of the Protestant Church, published the KING JAMES

BIBLE. The British Empire became great. Many countries became Protestant. The United States, the mother-country's daughter, became even greater. The Latin tongue of the Roman pontiff was abolished, and soon English became the world language, the language of the Protestant Church.

Alas, 400 years after the founding of the Protestant Church, her heirs turned away from *the* 'Faith,' and returned to Babylon and the apostasy of the Roman Catholic Church. The British Sovereign, King James I, Defender of *the* Faith, gave the world the Bible. His son and heir, an ecumenical Prince, Defender of *'all faiths,'* *"who regarded not the God (capitalized in KJV) of his fathers"* (Dan.11:36-38) became like mighty Nimrod of Babylon. In Wales and London, he is represented on their Coats of Arms as the *Great Red Dragon*—the new *Pontifex Maximus* of the apostate <u>*Protestant*</u> Church, the coming arch-enemy of Jews and Christians.

<u>***Special note on 'Genealogies':***</u> Many good Christian authors have written that *"neither shall he regard the God of his fathers"* in Daniel 11:37 implies that antichrist will be a Jew or non-religious Jew. The Jews have long rejected Christ. Will they not now accept a counterfeit christ as their messiah? The false messiah shortly to deceive Israel is to *claim* to be a Jew from the tribe of the Lion of Judah ruling on the throne of David.

To deceive unbelieving Israel and apostate Christians he must therefore claim by *'genealogy'* that he is their king and messiah. All of Israel's genealogical records were kept in the Temple at Jerusalem before Jesus was crowned king. When Titus desolated Jerusalem in A.D. 70, the temple was utterly destroyed, and with it, the records were all burnt. They had to be, because there was *no more* a need for them. Jesus Christ is now Israel's eternal King. There is now not a Jew in the world who can prove he is Israel's Messiah other than the person of Jesus Christ whose royal lineage is recorded in the Gospels and Old Testament. The book of the *generation* of Jesus Christ in Matthew chapter one is *not* a genealogy. Certain individuals who should naturally have been included were *removed* by the Gospel writers. Jehoiakim's name was removed because he used his penknife to cut out three or four pages of the word of God (Jeremiah 36:20-30). Ahaziah was rejected because he inquired of Baal-zeebub, the god of Ekron (2 Kings 1:2-4) and did evil in the sight of the LORD (2 Kings 8:25-27). Joash was rejected because he left the house of the LORD God of their fathers, and served groves and idols (2 Chronicles 24:20). Amaziah was rejected because he did turn away from following the LORD (2 Chronicles 25:27). These men have *already been removed* from the Book of Life because of their wickedness. The account in Matthew one is *not* a natural genealogy. In Matthew 1:5, two *faithful Gentile* women (Rahab the harlot and Ruth) are included. This is why Matthew called his account the book of the *"generation"* of Jesus Christ—not a *gene*-alogy. This is why the apostle Paul warned Timothy and Titus to *'avoid genealogies'* in Timothy 1:4 and Titus 3:9. Both the Papacy and the British Monarchy claim through '*genealogy*' they descend from the tribe of Judah and rule upon the throne of David. What blasphemy!

Like the Pontiff-king of Egypt, Pharaoh, who got his name from Hebrew '*He-Ro`e*'—'*Roe*' meaning a 'shepherd,' and the French '*Roi,*' a king, whence the

adjective *'Royal'*—whence the Latin *'Rex'* and *'Regal'*—
came the New Testament *'Herod'* *[a type of antichrist]*
and his brother's wife *'Herodias'* *[a type of antichrist's
wife, the Earth goddess]*—who required the head of John
the Baptist in a charger—came the final earthly Pontiff-
king of England—and thus, our Royal *Hero Maximus*,
the final World Babylonian Shepherd-King.

At the end of the 19th century/early 20th century, the
Processional Way and Ishtar Gate were excavated and
taken from Babylon and brought to the Pergamon Museum
in Berlin. The two man-headed bull statues that stood
on either side of the gate, the symbols of Marduk/Baal,
were brought to the British Museum in London. The
seat (throne) of the Babylonian king Bel-shaz-zar (called
the Pergamon Altar) was removed by German
archaeologists and transported to the Pergamon Museum
in Berlin.

It was the Pergamon Altar that gave Hitler his devilish
power during the Second World War. At the end of the
war it was removed and taken to Russia, but has since
been returned to the Pergamon Museum in Berlin. Its
return coincided with the Reunification of Germany, the
moving of Germany's new seat of Government from
Bonn back to Berlin, back into the newly renovated old
Nazi Reichstag Building, replete with its new giant Nazi
Prussian Eagle and symbol of Jupiter. If the Pergamon
Altar continues to reside in Berlin, (as it still does, as
at July 2000), this will undoubtedly be the global 'seat'
of power of Satan in the New Millennium. (Rev.2:13).

Protestant Germany *founded* the Reformation. Berlin
in German means 'small bear'—Berlin was founded by
Albert the Bear. Berlin's Coat of Arms is a 'bear.' United
in a coalition with Russia (the 'big bear'). The beast's

'feet of the *bear*' of Revelation 13:2.

Protestant Britain, that *promulgated* the Reformation, that enabled the common man to read God's word in English. The power that gave the nations a world language and Bible. (The British 'lion')—Her Sovereign is of German descent, her ceremonial soldiers still wear Roman 'red-coats,' and her hierarchical system is predominantly Roman. From her comes the *spokesperson* with 'a mouth speaking great things and blasphemies,' the 'mouth of a *lion*' of Revelation 13:2.

Protestant United States of America, the *greatest* Christian missionary country the world has ever seen. With a Protestant church on every corner, scattered throughout the cosmopolitan nation, made up of peoples from every nation on earth. (The 'leopard')—Her flag was worn by Pharaoh, the high priest, in Egypt, in the form of a *leopard-skin,* with spots covered with five-pointed stars, like Tutankhamen, whose ecclesiastical chair-seat was covered with leopard-skin and backed by Horus—the American eagle and sun-god. Tutankhamen was buried with two leopard-skin mantles adorned with five-pointed stars. His sarcophagus was lined with five-pointed stars. His crook was found with the figure of a leopard's head. His throne chair arms incorporated two leopard heads, whose head and mask was surrounded by stripes symbolizing the sun—the *Star-Spangled Banner,* the *Stars and Stripes* of the flag of the United States of America. America is the *main body* of the final global beast symbolized by the *'leopard'* of Revelation 13:2.

These great apostate *Protestant* Christian nations finally dominate the beastly world system of Revelation: "And I stood upon the sand of the sea, and I saw a beast rise up out of the sea, having seven heads and ten horns, and upon his horns ten crowns, and upon his heads the name of blasphemy. And the beast which I saw was like unto a *leopard*, and his feet were as the feet of a *bear*, and his mouth as the mouth of a *lion*: and the *dragon* gave him his power, and his *seat* and great authority." (Rev.13:1-2) ....And out of the once great <u>Protestant Church</u> and these *three formerly God-fearing great Protestant nations* came the great red *Dragon!*

<u>Charles, 'a man.'</u> Nimrod was worshipped as *a man* in Babylon. Aesculapius was worshipped as *a man* in Pergamos. ['*gamos*' means 'marriage' in Greek. *'Per'* in 'Pergamos' conveys a bad sense as in *'perfidia.'* *'Per'* is related to the Latin word *'perversus.'* Pergamos can thus be interpreted to mean *'perverted-marriage.'* In English the word 'perverse' encompasses a wide range of meanings such as corrupt, diverting from the true intent or object, *an <u>apostate</u>* and one who is sexually perverted.] The Pope was worshipped as *a man* in Rome. Goliath, the *champion*, was worshipped as *a man* by the Philistines (Palestinians) in Israel—and Judas Iscariot, whose name from its Hebrew roots literally means, *a man* of Kerioth from Judah. Kerioth was a town in Judah. 'Kerioth' in Hebrew means 'building' from a root that relates to the building's *'flooring.'* Remember Jesus' parable about the wise man who built his house upon the rock, and the foolish man who built his house upon the *sand* (latin: 'arena') (*Matt.7:24-27*) and *earth (Adam-George) (Luke 6:49)*. Judas was the one who *betrayed* Jesus. In late June 1990, Prince Charles spent three nights at Cirencester Hospital after *breaking his right arm* playing polo. In late October 1990, the plaster cast worn by the Prince of Wales was raffled off and raised 1700 pounds towards repairing the roof of the Church of St. Thomas of Canterbury at Kingswear, in Devon. In Jeremiah 48:24-25, there is a *broken arm on Kerioth* and in Zechariah 11:17, there is a *bad arm* on the false shepherd. The whole of Zechariah 11 is a prophesy of Judas Iscariot, who is a type of the great betrayer, antichrist. The scriptures are very precise! The betrayal of Christ was, and still is, an "inside job." Like Hitler, Charles loves *buildings* and *architecture,* and considers himself a great *painter.* Finally, in English, *Charles* means '*a man.*' In Hebrew 'iysh' means '*a man,*' connected to words like "Adam, Edom, Esau, earth, red," and in the KJV '*iysh*' translated *champion* is used to describe Goliath. British-Israelite Freemasons claim 'Brit-ish' is Hebrew meaning, *Covenant Man.* The word for '*a man*' in Latin is *Carolus,* in Italian *Carlo,* in Spanish *Carlos,* in French *Charles,* in German *Karl or Carl.* Traditionally 'Charles' as a name had great popularity in France and Germany, primarily due to *Charles* the Great or *Charlemagne.*

Charlemagne—Charles: Emperor of the Holy Roman Empire

Charlemagne [Charles I or Charles the Great] (742—814 A.D.) was crowned the *first* emperor of the Holy Roman Empire by Pope Leo III. On Christmas Day, the birthday of the sun-god, Baal (Jupiter, Zeus), in 800 A.D., the Pope placed the crown of the Caesars on the head of Charlemagne. Then the assembled people shouted: "Long life and victory to Charles Augustus the *crowned of God,* the great peace-giving Emperor of the Romans."

In crowning him, the 'Holy Father' usurped not only the title, but the authority of God the father—fulfilling Ezekiel 28:1-6 to the letter. In this very act the 'Vicar of Christ' confessed that he, himself, had "no king but Caesar." In reality, the Pope made himself a counterfeit of *'God the Father,'* and the Emperor a counterfeit of *'God the Son.'* The author of *Roman & European Mythologies, page 102,* says the word *'Caesar'* came from *'aesar'* which meant *'god'* in the old Etruscan language.

The crowning of Charlemagne commenced a union of Church and State that was to be described from the twelfth century onwards as the 'Holy Roman Empire.' It continued to exist, in name, until 1806, during which period it was held that every rightful emperor must be crowned at Rome by the pope. The title 'emperor' was an honorary one, conferred on the leading *'prince'* of Western Europe. This empire lasted for a thousand years and was the model for Hitler's thousand years' Reich.

Charles V (1500—1558 A.D.) was the *last* emperor of the Holy Roman Empire crowned by the Pope. He was crowned with great pomp at Bologna by Pope Clement in 1530. Charles totally failed to grasp the significance of the Protestant Reformation. All over Germany voices were raised in angry protest against the Roman Catholic Church—its wealth, its abuses, its corruption, its immoralities.

The Reformation movement, led by Martin Luther, was growing rapidly. Charles refused to condemn Luther unheard, despite the urgings of Pope Leo. He summoned him to the assembly at Worms, where Luther refused to recant saying that he would not act against his conscience.

There was nothing more that Charles could do and

Luther was outlawed. A month later the famous Edict of Worms forbade the preaching of new doctrines.

But it was too late. The light of the gospel of Christ in German hearts had broken the bondage of Rome. Soon the Reformation spread to other nations. The reigning years of the Roman emperors were numbered.

On 30 September, 1558, clasping his wife's crucifix in his hands, the *last* of the great Holy Roman emperors passed away. The Protestant Reformation had truly begun. The reign of the Roman emperors was finished—or so the Protestants thought. What they didn't understand was that the emperor had died, but his '*spirit*' lived on. The subject became very esoteric and subtle. It can best be briefly illustrated by retracing some of the history of the royal heraldry of Britain. Our account comes from *Royal Heraldry Beasts and Badges of Britain* by J.P. Brooke-Little, page14:

[George I, a great-grandson of James I, was not only Elector of Hanover, that is one of those princes who elected the *Holy Roman Emperor*, but also Duke of Brunswick and Luneburg. So, to symbolize his German dominions and dignities, he substituted German arms for the English and Scottish arms in the fourth quarter of the post-1707 royal arms.

The new coat was divided into three. In the first third were the two golden lions passant guardant on red of Brunswick. In the second third was shown a blue lion on a golden background spattered with red hearts: the arms of Luneburg. In the lower third the white horse of Hanover galloped in a red field. In the centre, on a small red shield was a representation of the *Crown of Charlemagne*, the badge of the *Arch-Treasurer of the Holy Roman Empire*, **_an office held by George._**

These arms were used by the first three Georges until 1801 when, because of the Act for Union with Ireland, the royal arms were altered yet again. On this occasion the royal arms of France, symbol of an ancient and hollow pretension, were finally removed. The arms of England were placed in the first and fourth quarters, those of Scotland in the second quarter and the harp of Ireland in the third. The German arms were placed on a shield in the centre of the royal arms. This shield was ensigned by the Electoral Bonnet, a crimson cap turned up with ermine, symbol of the electoral dignity.

After the ultimate defeat of Napoleon at Waterloo, the Congress of Vienna, in 1815, resettled the frontiers of Europe. The old Electorate of Hanover was made into a Kingdom, the Holy Roman Empire being no more. George III became the first King of Hanover and in 1816 an arched crown was substituted for the electoral bonnet in the royal arms.

King George IV and William IV, both kings of Hanover, used the same arms. But, when William IV died in 1837 and was succeeded by his niece Victoria, the crowns were divided. A woman could not rule in Hanover, so that the crown passed to William's next living brother, Ernest Duke of Cumberland and Queen Victoria removed the German arms from the royal arms. The result was the royal arms as we know them today.]

Thus, the office of the Emperor and Arch-Treasurer of the Holy Roman Empire, is _still held_ by the British Monarchy today—a monarchy that outwardly masquerades as Protestant and British, but is secretly more Roman Catholic and German. In fact, Prince Charles is a _direct descendant_ of Charlemagne and Frederick Barbarossa.

The European Union is Roman Catholic right to the

core. The Maastricht monster is growing into the 'beast' of Revelation chapter thirteen. It envisions a One World Holy Roman Empire Government, encompassing *every* nation on earth, ruled from Europe, and encompassing Russia and the United States of America.

The symbol of the *"euro"* (European Currency Unit) is the letter **"C"** through which are struck two horizontal bars **"="**. The letter **"C"** represents **Charles,** the coming Holy Roman Empire Emperor—the incarnation of the Babylonian sun-god. The **"="** cross-bars represent the number six, Castor and Pollux, the mother-earth goddess (more about Castor & Pollux later). The *euro* is the currency unit of the *Arch-Treasurer* of the Holy Roman Empire. Accordingly, on the face of the 50 *ecu* coin (1987) is a bust of Charles V, the *last* emperor of the Holy Roman Empire.

As Protestants in the formally great Protestant countries like Britain, Germany and the United States of America give up the faith of their early forefathers, their sovereignty is rapidly diminishing. In its place, will come the new Dark Ages and enslavement of the *'beast'* of Revelation.

In a Bavarian myth, Charlemagne was said to be in an upright position in his tomb at Aachen with his white beard still growing. When his beard had three times encircled the stone table before which he was sitting, the end of the world would come. That time is fast approaching.

In German mythology Charlemagne was said, like Frederick Barbarossa, to be awaiting a resurrection when he would win back his empire. Charlemagne is coming to life again!

At the 'progressive governance' summit of

government leaders, held in *Berlin* (remember—the Pergamon altar) in June 2000, Bill Clinton became the first U.S. President to receive the prestigious **Charlemagne Prize** for his contribution to *European* unity. In 1993 Queen Elizabeth II conferred the Honorary Knight Grand Cross (GCB) upon Sir George Bush, almost as soon as he left his presidential office. This is the highest rank the Queen can give anyone who is not her official subject. With other high ranking British Monarchy controlled leaders like Sir Henry Kissinger, Gen. Sir Norman Schwarzkopf, Gen. Sir Colin Powell, Sir Caspar Weinberger etc., and a Federal Reserve Bank that is privately owned and directed from London and Frankfurt, America is now *totally* controlled from Europe.

In the film *Gladiator*, Maximus, while fighting in the arena of the Colosseum, is wearing a Roman gladiator's vest. On the breast-plate is a Christmas fir-tree symbolizing the new-born god Baal-berith. Next to the tree is a woman and child, the Virgin-mother and child, the Babylonian Isis and Horus, the Roman goddess Fortuna and Jupiter her son. Surrounding the tree, woman and child, are two white horses and two winged-lions. The white horses are the symbol of the *badge* of the Saxon kings of England, the symbol of the *House of Hanover*. They are the ancient symbols of Odin (Jupiter). The two winged-lions are the Roman equivalent of the two 'horned man-bull statues' that stood on either side of the Ishtar gate in Babylon that represented Nimrod-Baal—the Babylonian antichrist.

If Prince Charles of Great Britain were to be crowned by the Pope when he becomes king—he would likely be crowned **Charles VI**, *Emperor and Arch-Treasurer of the Holy Roman Empire*. Since the *last* emperor crowned by the Pope was Charles V, the next Charles naturally would be Charles VI—*number 6* in scripture being the number of '*a man.*' He would live in London, but rule from Berlin [provided the Pergamon Altar continues to reside in the Pergamon Museum].

In February 2000, Prince Charles announced he wanted to be called *King George* when he ascended the throne because the first two kings called Charles "have tarnished images" *[N.Z.Herald, Feb.14, 2000]*. Only time will tell what his final name will be, but needless to say, the momentous events quickly transpiring in the Middle East arena will soon reveal the true identity of the Babylonian 'prince of peace' and 'man of sin.' When he brings his 'peace' to Jerusalem, be it for such a short period, as is indicated in scripture, he will literally be *worshipped* by every man, woman and child on earth who do not have Jesus Christ as their true Prince of Peace and Saviour.

The cheering crowds of the world 'Colosseum' will worship him as their '*Champion Gladiator*' and, as such, the 'people' may very well *name* him themselves. He may have no choice. The leader of the World Church will crown him with the '*will*' of the people.

David and Goliath: David and Goliath are the *real* 'gladiatorial finalists' in the world Colosseum. David, in scripture, was made king *twice*. The first time he was made king he was crowned by '*some*' of the people. The second time he was made king he was crowned by '*all*' of the people. At Jesus' first coming, he was made king by '*some*' of the people of Israel. At his second coming, he will be made king by the '*whole*' House of Israel. Before David became king of Israel, he slew Goliath '*twice.*' First, with a stone from a brook, then secondly, he slew Goliath with the giant's *own* sword. Goliath is the *only* person in scripture referred to as being a *'champion.'* The word *'champion'* translated from Hebrew *'iysh'* literally means *'a man.'* Goliath's height was six cubits and a span. The weight of his spear's head was six hundred shekels. He had six pieces of armour. Goliath was sealed with three sixes. His name appears exactly six times in scripture. Before Goliath there were *five* lords of the Philistines (Palestinians). Goliath was their *'champion'* and a *'sixth.'* David chose *'five'* smooth stones out of a brook. Each stone was symbolically reserved for each lord. This is why David slew Goliath *'twice.'* David slew Goliath first with one stone that was representative of what was in store for the *five* lords and enemies of Israel. Goliath was then slain a *second time* with his *own* sword. In all, there were five lords and one champion. The great *champion* was the *sixth*.

In all, there were *five* emperors of the Holy Roman Empire that were called *'a man'* *'Charles.'* All these emperors were enemies of Israel, Jews and Christians. The last one coming soon will be the final *'champion.'* Like Goliath, he is the *sixth*. Like the *'champion'* of the Philistines and all those who follow him, he will be killed with his *own sword* (Rev.13:10).

The *five smooth stones* that David chose out of the brook were untouched by man. They were the same as the *'stone'* *'cut out of the mountain without hands'* that smote Nebuchadnezzar's great image (of 'a man') in Daniel 2:34,45. That *stone* is Jesus Christ. At his *'first coming,'* Jesus the son of David, slew Nebuchadnezzar's great image. Through preaching the gospel of *faith* in Christ, Babylon, Medo-Persia, Grecia and Rome were dead. By the time of Constantine, over one half the entire population of the Roman Empire were Christians. These four once great empires "became like the chaff of the summer threshing-floors; and the wind carried them away, *that no place was found for them:* and the stone that smote the image became a great mountain, and filled the whole earth." (Daniel 2:35)—Christianity then ruled the world, and these four great world empires were replaced by the Christian Church.

'After' Nebuchadnezzar had died, Daniel had a dream and vision of four great beasts (kingdoms) that would arise *still in the future* heralding Christ's *'second coming'* (Daniel 7). These four great beasts were; a *lion,* a *bear,* a *leopard* and a *fourth terrible beast with ten horns.* No longer does God now view the leading world nations as simply an image of a man. He now portrays them as great wild beasts. These are the great apostate Christian nations of today. This is the time in which we are now living. The first four world kingdoms, beginning with Nebuchadnezzar, leading up to Christ's *first coming,* were but 'shadows' of the final four leading up to the Lord's *second coming.*

These great apostate Christian nations dominate the beast of Revelation 13. These are the principal final world powers. Britain (the lion), Germany with links with Russia (the bear), United States of America (the leopard) and the European Union, the head of the World Government (the fourth terrible beast with ten horns). Before David slew Goliath he said:

*"And David said unto Saul, Thy servant kept his father's sheep, and there came a **lion,** and a **bear,** and took a lamb out of the flock: And I went out after him, and*

smote him, and delivered it out of his mouth: and when he arose against me, I caught him by his beard, and smote him, and slew him. Thy servant slew both the lion and the bear: and this uncircumcised Philistine shall be as one of them, seeing he hath defied the armies of the living God." (I Samuel 17:34-36).

Before David fought the Philistine he said;

"Thou comest to me with a sword, and with a spear, and with a shield: but I come to thee in the name of the LORD of hosts, the God of the armies of Israel, whom thou hast defied. This day will the LORD deliver thee into mine hand; and I will smite thee, and take thine head from thee; and I will give the carcases of the host of the Philistines this day unto the fowls of the air, and to the wild beasts of the earth; that all the earth may know that there is a God in Israel. And all this assembly shall know that the LORD saveth not with sword and spear: for the battle is the LORD'S, and he will give you into our hands." (I Samuel 17:45-47).

The Israeli Defence Force, led by a king Saul as at the present, will *not* save Israel from the full force of the United Nations. Ultimately, Israel's salvation will *not* come through 'sword and spear,' but only by *faith* in the son of David, Jesus Christ.

Charles—The Suffering Servant: The Old Testament prophesied that Jesus Christ would come as a suffering *'Servant'* and *'Prince'*(Ezekiel 34:23-24). Philippians 2:7-8 says;

"But [Jesus] made himself of no reputation, and took upon him the form of a *'servant,'* and was made in the likeness of men: And being found in fashion as *a man*, he humbled himself, and became obedient unto death, even the death of the cross." Jesus, the Prince of life and Saviour (Acts 3:15, 5:31) said, "But he that is greatest among you shall be your *servant*" (Matt.23:11). He warned, "...whosoever killeth you will think he doeth God *service" (John 16:2)*.

The Prince of Wales' personal motto is German 'Ich dien'—'*I serve*'.

"And all that dwell upon the earth shall *worship* him, whose names are not written in the book of life of the Lamb slain from the foundation of the world." (Revelation 13:8).

__Five Cities and Ten Kings:__ The MAIN PROVISIONS OF THE CONSTITUTION FOR THE FEDERATION OF EARTH, adopted at the 1977 session of the World Constituent Assembly and revised at the 1991 session of the World Constitution and Parliament Association recommended the following: (a) The Earth be divided up into *ten* Magna-Regions for elections and administration. (b) *Five* World Capitals be established in *five* continental divisions with one being the Primary Capital and the others the Secondary Capitals.

There were *five* cities of the plain allied with Sodom and Gomorrah (Gen.14:8). There were *five* cities of the Philistines that fought against Israel (I Sam. 6:17). In the last days, the World Government Gentile beast that rises up against Israel will have *ten* horns and *ten* kings (Rev. 13:1, 17:12) ruling over the *ten* Magna-Regions of the world. These kings will rule from *five* Continental World Capitals.

The ancient *five* cities of the Philistines were Ashdod, Gaza, Askelon, Gath and Ekron. These locations are still revered by the Palestinians today and sometimes featured in the world news. They are a 'type' of the soon to come principal *five* world capital cities. Goliath is a 'type' of antichrist, the coming champion warrior of the Palestinians and World King.

James, a name developed from the Hebrew word '*Jacob.*' *James*, a book in the Bible, the son of Zebedee, a name of a brother of our Lord. *James I*, the British sovereign who gave the world the King James Bible. There are 440 churches dedicated to him in Britain alone. *Jamestown*, the *first* permanent English settlement in America (1607), was founded in recognition of this great British sovereign. His bible and language made America great.

Prince Charles reveres his forefather's King James Bible version because of its majestic and poetic language—not because he believes it. Ironically, his office is situated in St. James Palace—but tragically, "he regardeth not the God of his fathers" (Daniel 11:37). What shall befall this man?

Philip a name which comes from Greek, means 'lover of horses.' Interestingly, Saint George is usually portrayed riding on a white horse while slaying the dragon.

Castor and Pollux were the Roman equivalent of the Babylonian constellation of Gemini, represented as two small children, the pagan substitution of Jacob and Esau. Two important stars in the constellation of Gemini still bear the names of Castor and Pollux. The stories concerning Gemini, Castor and Pollux, as well as Romulus and Remus in the founding of Rome all have a very close resemblance to the stories involved with St. George and the Dragon.

Castor and Pollux were the tutelary deities of

navigation, sailors and the *'patrons of horsemen.'* Castor
had been specially 'chosen' because of his specialty as
a *'horseman.'* Like Castor, the Prince of Wales is an
expert *'horseman.'*

All pagan religions of the world worship 'twin gods'
or 'twin brothers.' Always one is inferior to the other.
Pollux must assign half his immortality to Castor, Zethus
dominates Amphion, Romulus kills Remus and so on.
Always one is sacrificed, and the other becomes a founding
hero. This perversion of the true scriptural characters is
perpetuated in St. George and the Dragon and *'Maximus
and Commodus.'* All of these pagan accounts are
counterfeits of the true biblical stories of 'Cain slaying
Abel' and 'Jacob being preferred above Esau.'

The White Horse of Jupiter: In Rome, Castor and
Pollux rode on white horses. The white horse was sacred
to Jupiter, and once a year the consul, clad in white
robes, rode to the Capitol to adore Jupiter as the sun-
god.

It is said that there will be one more incarnation of
Vishnu, when he will carry the sword of justice and
ride on a white horse. The horse was used by the Hindus
instead of the Ram. Aries or the Ram is the constellation
in which the sun starts its zodiacal journey each year,
the ram or horse signifying the opener of new thought,
the dawn of a new era. Hence to ride the white horse
means to begin a new kingdom on earth of joy and
happiness. When Mohammed comes again, Moslems
believe he will ride on a white horse called Alborac.

Buddha is said to have been borne to earth on a
white elephant. Osiris and Zeus are spoken of as white
bulls. St. George is nearly always depicted riding on a
white horse while slaying the dragon. This is not the

white horse Jesus is riding on in Revelation 19:11. It is none other than the white horse sacred to Jupiter. More appropriately, it is similar to the *'pale horse of death'* of Revelation 6:8—a horse of death upon which Jupiter (incarnated in the emperor) sat while watching the Christians being martyred in the arena of the Roman Colosseum.

The pagan practice of 'riding the white horse' is the ultimate rebellion of Jesus Christ's triumphal entry into Jerusalem. "Rejoice greatly, O daughter of Zion; shout, O daughter of Jerusalem: behold, thy King cometh unto thee: he is just, and having salvation; lowly, and riding upon an ass, and upon a colt the foal of an ass." (Zechariah 9:9) "And the multitudes that went before, and that followed, cried saying, Hosanna to the son of David: Blessed is he that cometh in the name of the Lord; Hosanna in the highest."(Matthew 21:9) Will not antichrist, the coming counterfeit 'prince of peace' of the Middle East arena, be received in Jerusalem in a similar manner?

Centuries of tradition have dictated the British heir to the throne or British Sovereign ride a white horse in the ceremony called *'Trooping the Colour.'* Anna Sproule's book *Prince Charles*, page 52, provides an excellent photo of Prince Charles riding a white horse 'Trooping the Colour' in June, 1975. After Trooping the Colour, Prince Charles, as Colonel of the Welsh Guards, was photographed riding his white horse outside Buckingham Palace. He is dressed in Royal regalia, including his 'Roman Red-coat' and badge of St. George (Jupiter) pinned over his heart. Page 61 of the same book reveals a full-page photograph of Prince Charles making a pre-flight inspection check on an *HMS Hermes* navy helicopter. On his right shoulder is a large badge of a *Red Dragon*, the symbol of Wales and 845 Squadron.

The British custom of 'Trooping the Colour' originated in Rome. After the Roman monarchy was replaced by a republican form of government towards the close of the sixth century B.C., the consuls who replaced the king *jointly* exercised the full imperium of the kings that previously ruled. However, their tenure of office was restricted to one year.

In the early history of the Republic, in a state of civil emergency or a quarrel between the consuls, a *dictator* was appointed on the recommendation of the senate. The dictator in turn nominated as his subordinate officer the *'Master of the Horse'* (*Magister Equitum*). Both held office for six months. The dictator superseded all other authority during his tenure of office, and originally there was no appeal from him to the people. He had sole command of the army.

It would appear the Prince of Wales' superlative training as an expert *'horseman,'* and his distinguished military career, have prepared him well for his new role in the World Republic—a role and destiny where at some point in history he will inevitably be voted *'Man of the Year,'*—as he follows the footsteps of the consuls, and rides the white horse of Jupiter into a New Dark Age—the reborn unholy Roman Empire.

Arthur: The etymology of this name is a little uncertain. Some say it is derived from Celtic *artos* 'a bear.' In Irish *'art'* means 'a stone.' The earliest recorded example of the name Arthur occurs (as Arturius) in Adamnan's life of St. Columba, where it is the name of an Irish prince killed in 596 A.D. The earliest mention of King Arthur is in Nennius (fl. 796). In about 500 A.D., mythical King Arthur set about the founding of his Order of Chivalry to which he gave the name of the 'Round Table.' He adopted St. George, that Constantine had declared the *Champion of Christendom*, as the Patron and Protector of his Order of the Knights of the Round Table. The Welsh title of the *'Gorsedd'* (*'gor'* = great *'sedd'* = seat, great seat or throne of the monarch), by which the Windsor Table-mound is known, is connected to the tradition that the *'Gorsedd'* comes from Aedd Mawr's organization of famous Druids, Bards and Ovates, founded in 1,000 B.C. In pagan Britain, pre-Christian times, Druidical meetings were held on *table mounds* on high places in the *Face of the Sun*. King Edward III, in re-founding the British Order, went to great pains to preserve the sanctity of the Arthurian Table-Mound, by encircling the *'Gorsedd'* with a 'Round Tower.' *Gorsedds* were the symbol of the whole earth. Arthur and his legendary Knights of the Round Table are the Druid counterfeit of Jesus and his twelve disciples. The British Sovereign, as head of the Order of the Garter and head of the Knights of the Round Table, is also head of World Freemasonry. As such, the Masonic *'Great Architect of the Universe'* is incarnated in the character that sits at the head of the Round Table.

Before <u>CHARLES V</u> was crowned Emperor of the Holy Roman Empire by Pope Clement in 1530, he was installed as a Knight of the Round Table in St. George's Chapel and the Windsor Round Tower, on St. George's Day, 1522. In company with his illustrious guest, Henry VIII spent a week with Charles at Winchester Castle in order that the King-Emperor might behold the British King Arthur's original Round Table in the gable of the Great Hall of England's Old Parliament House. It was on this special occasion that the Tudor monarch ordered this ancient relic of chivalry to be painted and decorated as we see it today, in green and white (green being the colour of the livery of the British Order). The Red Rose in the centre of the table represents the Tudor Rose of the Monarch. It is closely associated with the badge (red cross) of St. George. In high degree Masonry, the Tudor Rose represents the union of the Rose of England with the Rose of Sharon.

The Rose of Sharon originated in the city of Lydda, the mythical birth-place of St. George. Lydda (or Hebrew Lod or Ludd) is situated in the fertile plain of Sharon, twelve miles from the port of Joppa or Jaffa. The plain of Sharon has always been recognized as a rich and fertile area in Israel. Traditionally, it has been endowed with orchards of olive, fig, pomegranate, mulberries and sycamore. The Arabs call this the 'green district' or 'the garden of Palestine.' From this birth-place Saint George gained his mythical name, the *'Evergreen green One.'* The 'One' who is represented by the Rose of Sharon is the monarch who heads the Knights of the Round Table. In reality, this infamous character is the *incarnation* of the Roman sun-god—Jupiter!

The Palestinian flag is green, white, red and black. Green, white and red are associated with St. George and the Rose of Sharon. Black is the colour of the priests of Saturn. St. George is thus a modern 'Goliath' of the Palestinians.

King Arthur and the Knights of the Round Table
The organizational structure of the Catholic Church, British Monarchy and Council of Europe is exclusively 'Roman.' The Imperial Roman system was perpetuated and *improved* by the Vatican, but the Monarchy *perfected* it.

Originally, the people of the Republic elected magistrates to rule over them. From these officials, consuls and praetors were appointed who held power of rule (*imperium*) that was virtually absolute (except in the condemnation of a citizen to death). After their term of office these ex-magistrates were usually chosen to fill vacancies in the *Council of Elders* (Senate), which thus became a repository of political wisdom and experience.

Gradually, the senators became corrupt and apathetic. Instead of seriously debating the questions submitted, the senators would invariably vote steadily for what they believed the emperor would desire. They refused to accept responsibility, and threw the whole burden back upon his shoulders. Thus the emperors were compelled to seek advice and assistance elsewhere, and in course of time the Senate was ousted by a new body, the *Privy Council*, composed of men chosen by the emperor to consider his imperial questions. Thus the Senate became little more than the town-council. *[This process is presently happening to the Senate in America. During the reign of Commodus (George Bush Jnr), the new President of the United States—the U.S. Senate is to be converted into little more than a town-council, that will be ruled, not by Americans, but by a new body, a type of World Privy Council.]*

Graccus passed a series of laws designed to consolidate the body of public contractors, rich merchants and financiers as a political force in opposition to the Senate. These men were drawn from the social class called the *'Knights'* (or *'Equestrian Order'*), titles which originally implied service in the cavalry, but which long had ceased to have any military significance. Their

Witness. This is what Fricker claims in his book:

"I was once a little boy in the Holy Land at the time of Christ. I had later been trained in Heaven before being sent back to Earth, via Tottenham, to conduct a healing mission—It's not the first time I've been here—I used to run after Jesus, touching his clothing because I loved him so much. *That's why God sent me back to Earth as a miracle worker, just like Christ.*"

According to John Dale, Prince Charles believes this book to the letter.

Many of Fricker's claims are embodied in the spiritualistic film, *ET.*

The Extra Terrestrial (1982), directed by Steven Spielberg, is about an alien (ET) who becomes stranded on Earth, three million light years from home. During his sojourn on Earth, ET miraculously forms a special bond with a boy named Elliot (an allusion to Elijah in Malachi 4:5). The 'spirit' of the alien enters the little boy before ET dies, then ET miraculously comes alive and returns home. The whole story is a satanic counterfeit of the prophesied Second Coming of Jesus Christ.

In Revelation 16:13, John saw three unclean spirits like *frogs* come out of the mouth of the dragon, beast and false prophet. Like many aliens, ET both '*looks*' and '*croaks*' like a *frog.* ET represents the Devil and Elliot, Antichrist.

On June 20, 1997, the *New Zealand TV Guide*, page 119, published the following statement: 'Steven Spielberg has *framed* a handwritten note from Prince Charles which thanks the director for all the enjoyment the royal family have derived from ET. Apparently, they've watched it more than *thirty* times.'

Walking in the footsteps of the Messiah, and with a

thinly-veiled comparison with Moses, *a man* is soon to come who believes himself to be the literal, physical, spiritual, re-incarnation of Jesus Christ.

Charles: The 'Pope' in the Protestant 'Vatican:' Westminster Abbey—or more correctly, the Collegiate Church of St. Peter, was designed after St. Peter's in Rome. The Abbey has been dedicated to St. Peter himself, in precisely the same way as its Vatican equivalent. The Abbey's stones, relics and icons tell a story of English history covering a period of more than nine centuries. It is the world's greatest Christian temple that symbolizes the relentless struggle between Roman Catholicism and Protestantism. Over three thousand famous people have been buried within its walls. Apart from Edward V and Edward VIII, every sovereign has been crowned in it since 1066. To the English Church, this temple is what Solomon's temple was to Israel. Every sovereign crowned in this Abbey is crowned and anointed with oil in precisely the same way as David and Solomon and the ancient kings of Judah. These British monarchs actually believe they are Christ's representatives and regents here on earth, just like the Pope!

The Chapter House of Westminster Abbey was used as a meeting place for the King's Great Council in the 14th century where great feudal Lords, powerful Knights, Freemen and Burgesses met. The 'Commons' were summoned to this House, and from this famous location the English Parliament and parliamentary system evolved. Around the inside walls of the Chapter House are some notable paintings depicting scenes in the book of Revelation including; The Last Judgment, The Great Beast, The Lamb and his Company, The Whore of Babylon, The War of Armageddon and The New

Jerusalem. Perhaps the choice and location of these prophetic paintings is not just a coincidence?

The Jerusalem Chamber in the Abbey has special significance for Protestants and the English Bible. Here the committee met that was responsible for the Authorized King James Version of the Bible, published in 1611, as did those who worked on the Revised version (1881-1885, revised again 1946-952), the New English Bible (1961-70) and the Revised English Bible with the Apocrypha (1970).

Westminster Abbey is strictly known as a 'Royal Peculiar.' This is the Sovereign's Church. When Henry VIII broke with Rome, he broke with the Pope as head of the Church, but _not spiritually_ with St. Peter. As Britain gives up her sovereignty, and the Protestant Church rapidly apostatizes and develops closer relationships with Rome, like a dog returning to its vomit, the Pope or his representatives may very well regain their former power over the English Church (or vice-versa).

Around 1990, the Protestant King James Bible on the Great Lectum of Westminster Abbey was _replaced_ with the spurious Roman Catholic inspired Revised English Bible with Apocrypha—much to the chagrin of Protestant fundamentalist Christians. This blasphemous act was symptomatic of a greater evil taking place in the mind of the Sovereign.

Each year the 'Commonwealth Service' is held in the Abbey and is attended by the Queen, Prince Charles and the Commonwealth heads of Government. Traditionally, as part of the service, each representative has been required to read a portion of scripture from the Bible. Since about 1990, the Queen has permitted the Commonwealth heads of Government to read passages of script from their own books of religion—now including the Koran! King James, who is buried in the Abbey, would be turning in his grave if he could hear what is happening!

Two great inscriptions may be found in the Abbey that epitomize the contrast between truth and error in the Church. The first can be found on the memorial tablet of William Tyndale (1490-1536), who translated the Holy Scriptures into the language of the English people. Before he was burned at the stake in 1536, praying "Lord, open the King of England's eyes," he said:

> "*There is none other way into the Kingdom of Life* than through persecution and suffering of pain and of very death after the example of Christ."

The second inscription is written upon the wall above the *High Altar* as follows:

> "The kingdoms of this world are become the *kingdoms of our Lord, and of his Christ.*"

The <u>last</u> words of Revelation 11:15, *"and he shall reign for ever and ever"*—are <u>*missing!*</u>

Both the Pope and the British monarch claim to be ruling on the throne of David. They *both* claim to be Christ's descendants and supreme visible representatives on earth. They *both* claim to be ruling over the Kingdom of Heaven and the Kingdom of God on earth.

> "*And I beheld another beast coming up out of the earth; and he had two horns like a lamb, and he spake as a dragon.*" (Revelation 13:11)

What an apt description of the *leaders* of the apostate Church! One Roman Catholic horn and one Protestant horn, on a beast that looks like a lamb, but speaks as a *dragon*!

<u>*Charles: The Covenant Man*</u>: The 'covenant' mentioned in Daniel 9:27 that is prophesied to be "confirmed" with many for one week (possibly a week of seven years) is *probably* the *Jerusalem Covenant.* Time will very soon confirm if it is or not. On Jerusalem Day, May 19, 1993, the completed Covenant, after having been sent around the world for one year for signatures of approval, was presented back to Israel's President Ezer Weizman for safekeeping.

The Covenant was signed by the Speaker of the Knesset, Prime Minister, President of State of Israel, Chief Rabbi (Sephardi), Chief Rabbi (Ashkenazi), Mayor of Jerusalem and many others of the most important dignitaries in Israel. Contrary to the fact God has *already* made an *everlasting covenant* with his chosen people Israel, (Genesis 17:7) and he has promised *"I will never break my covenant with you"* (Judges 2:1-2) and he has commanded Israel *"not to make a covenant with anybody else"* (Exodus 23:32, Deuteronomy 7:2, Judges 2:1-2) this new man-made Covenant is an abominable addition to the Word of God.

In spite of the fact God has reserved Jerusalem *exclusively* for his 'Name' and his name only, these disbelieving Jews have entered into a covenant with death. The last part of the Jerusalem Covenant says:

"Each and every nation will live in it by its <u>own faith:</u> 'For all the nations will go forward, each with its <u>own Divine Name;</u> we shall go in the name of the Lord our God for ever and ever.' And in this spirit the Knesset

of the State of Israel has enacted a law: the places holy to the peoples of __all religions__ shall be protected from any desecration and from any restriction of free access to them."

Great *judgement* is to come upon Israel for compromising and disobeying the commandments of the Lord.

Israel, (and indeed, the entire world) is to enter a time of travail. The scriptures have prophesied a time is soon to come, when the LORD shall make Jerusalem *"a cup of trembling for all nations"* (Zechariah 12:2-3). Gradually the 'birth pangs will get stronger and stronger. The *Jerusalem Covenant* is precisely the sort of document that could be 'confirmed' by a Roman prince. According to the Jerusalem Post, on June 1, 2000, Israel formally became an associate member of the European Union. The stage is now being set for the *"prince"* of a revived Holy Roman Empire to bring peace to the Middle East after a terrible time of chaos. Only after everything else fails will he reluctantly step forward. Of course, he will be worshipped both by Jew and Arab alike as the world messiah—the hero Maximus of the Global Colosseum.

__Charles: Father of the Children of the World:__ *'Hitler Youth' and 'The Prince's Trust.'*

Psalm 146:3 "Put not your *trust* in *princes*, nor in the son of man, in whom there is no help."

Hitler disbanded all previous youth organizations and replaced them with his own *Hitler Youth (Hitler Jugend) (H.J.)*. This was the principal instrument of Nazi socialist education and pre-military training from which Hitler wanted to create a youth which was "as tough as leather, as hard as Krupp steel, as quick as grey-hounds." The state education institutions held a grip on citizens from childhood. All children were taught "to think nothing but German, to feel German and to behave German." The Fuhrer wanted a race of pure Aryans. (Literally, the word 'Aryan' means 'a noble lord of the soil').

German youth had been dragged up through the high unemployment during the Depression which led to suicide and despondency. Hitler gave them work and a meaningful purpose for living. He encouraged young people to help old ladies cross the street safely, have a community spirit, and generally help others in need. This gave them a pride in themselves and a hope for living.

Hitler Youth was divided up into sections with 'bonn' or district numbers. Each section offered a special service. For example, there was the Hitler Youth flight training section. The *'Landjahr Hitler Jugend,'* carried out environmental, agricultural and other land duties. To help foster pride in their divisions, many units featured names of honoured Nazis like Captain Berthold, a distinguished flying ace, or Horst Wessel, a famous martyr.

Under these alluring circumstances, it was easy for a naïve youth to receive the silver eagle of Jupiter as his badge of allegiance and sleeve insignia. In his ignorance, it was even easier to give his heart and soul to the Devil—and worship the Fuhrer.

Hitler Youth, however, was just schoolboy's stuff compared to what was to come. About forty years later, in Britain, during the early 70's—early 80's Prince Charles founded *The Prince's Trust* with a desire to help disadvantaged young people find employment and training. The objects of the Trust reflected Prince Charles' passionate desire that Britain should have a system of 'national community service,' not only a 'military service,' to help young people gain self discipline and motivation.

Since its inception and very humble beginnings, the Trust has now grown into the biggest voluntary seed-corn finance operation on earth. Its multi-cultural, global youth programmes in education, training, life skills development and job creation are now, by far, the most outstandingly successful in the world.

As a charitable trust, it deliberately keeps a low profile in the public arena. Behind the scenes however, it is a different matter. Now funded by national and international big-business sponsorship, and growing like wildfire, its *Youth Business Initiative* operates in sixteen different countries. The British division alone has over five hundred permanent staff and over eight thousand volunteers.

The first overseas branch of *The Prince's Trust* was launched in New Zealand by Countess Mountbatten (with video-link messages from HRH Prince Charles) on July 17, 1995. Being the Trust's guinea-pig for the world, New Zealand's four year experiment has targeted youth in the 11 to 25 year-old age bracket. A strategic alliance between the Trust, big-business and the Government has been formed. Commencing January 1, 2001, the Trust's programmes are planned to be gradually implemented by government departments including the police and the military. During early 2001, a national advertising campaign is scheduled to begin. Towards the end of 2001, a big international television advertising promotion is planned to commence from New Zealand with a 24 hr international rock concert 'Party in the

Park.' The plan is to telecast this concert live by satellite to the youth in every nation on earth. Among the chief sponsors are global telecom companies.

The aim is *not* to develop young people into good German citizens to respect the 'Fatherland' as did Hitler. Rather, now, the goal is totally *global* in character. Its one primary objective is designed to convert the youth of the world into good *'World-Citizens'* and members of one united *'Family of Nations'*—of course, with the help of a benevolent *family 'father'* at its head. Literally, *Jupiter* means *'father who helps.'*

When Prince Charles was invested Prince of Wales on July 1, 1969, he was given *The Gold Ring*—two *dragons* of gold clutching an amethyst. The ring officially symbolizes that the Prince is wedded to his country and is the *father of her children.* As the Prince of Wales expands his Trust throughout the world, his oath of office dictates he must become the *father* of the children of the world (*mother*-earth). The United Nations sponsored laws, arising from the *U.N. Convention Charter on Rights of the Child*, are being implemented with one sole purpose in mind—to surreptitiously *transfer* the biblical God-given rights of parents over their children—directly to the Prince of Darkness, the devilish Fuhrer *(father).*

John 8:44 explains that the *devil* is a 'father.' He is a substitute of our true Father in heaven. Jesus said to Philip, "Have I been so long time with you, and yet hast thou not known me, Philip? He that hath seen me hath seen the *Father*..." (John 14:9). Apostate Jews and Christians could well heed Jesus' warning, "But be not ye called *Rabbi*: for one is your Master, even Christ; and all ye are brethren. And call no man your *father* upon the earth: for one is your Father, which is in heaven.

Neither be ye called *masters*: for one is your Master, even Christ." (Matthew 23:8-10). Since 1725 the Chapel of King Henry VII in Westminster Abbey has been the chapel of the Most Honourable Order of the Bath. This Order of Chivalry goes back to the Middle Ages. The name of the Order is derived from the ancient practice of ceremonial bathing before the reception of knighthood. It is a Masonic witchcraft practice that substitutes genuine Christian baptism. The Prince of Wales is *Grand Master* of the Order.

Jesus *whole* ministry was to *children*. Jesus said to his disciples, "Verily I say unto you, Except ye be converted, and become as little *children*, ye shall not enter into the kingdom of heaven." (John 18:3). He continued, "But whoso shall offend one of these little ones which believe in me, it were better for him that a millstone were hanged about his neck, and that he were drowned in the depth of the sea. Woe unto the world because of offences! For it must needs be that offences come; but woe to *that man* by whom the offence cometh!" (John 18:6-7). Judas hanged himself. Hitler committed suicide. What now is to befall *that man* of sin who is soon to betray the children of the world?

If the pattern of events that brought Hitler to power is followed again in the future, the timing of the planned *international* publicity promotion campaign of *The Prince's Trust* towards the end of 2001 would tend to indicate there is soon a period of global chaos coming. First the Depression—then the Fuhrer.

The New Zealand logo for the Prince of Wales Trust (to be called *The Prince's Trust* from late 2000—early 2001) includes a crown surmounted by an inverted (upside down) *Crux Ansata (or Ankh)*. The *Crux Ansata* is perhaps the most common of all emblems found on Egyptian monuments, carried in the hand of almost every figure of a deity or priest. It is carried in the right-hand of the Egyptian gods Seth, Horus, Re-Harakti, Amun-Re, Bastet Khnum and the goddess Isis.

In Egypt and Babylon, the *Crux Ansata* was made up from the mystic *Tau* or cross that represented Tammuz. To identify Tammuz with the sun, the cross was surmounted with a coiled serpent above it. The simple *Tau* was called the 'Sign of Life' and when the circle, symbol of 'Eternity' was added, the completed symbol represented 'Eternal Life.'

The Pharaonic theory of sacrosanct monarch presented the king as god made manifest in the flesh. Pre-eminently, pharaoh was Re, the supreme ruler—the sun-god. Usually he was attired with a *Crux Ansata* because it symbolized his eternal reign. Hitler used the swastika and Maltese cross in a similar manner to symbolize his thousand year Reich. The inverted *Crux Ansata* was included in the hieroglyph name of Pharaohs Snefetu, Phiops II and Akhenaten.

The *Crux Ansata* was included in the hieroglyphic name of Pharaoh Ramesses II, who wore it with the other characters of his name on each shoulder. With the *Crux Ansata* on each shoulder and himself the incarnation of the sun-god *Tau*, he was, in fact, represented as the embodiment of the triple *Tau* (666). Most historians say Ramesses II was the Pharaoh who was ruling during the time of Moses at the institution of Israel's Passover. To Jews, Passover signifies the birth and salvation of Israel. The world's final satanic attack against the rebirth and re-gathering of Israel, the Jewish Passover and Jesus Christ and his followers, is thus to be led by a man who sees himself the incarnation of this particular Pharaoh.

The *Tau* cross was the symbol of the slain and risen sun-god, Tammuz, whom the women of Jerusalem were weeping for in Ezekiel 8:14-16. While the women wept, the men with their backs toward the temple of the LORD and their faces toward the east, worshipped the sun. For this abomination, the LORD slew all of the Tammuz worshippers in Jerusalem—men, women and children, old and young. Only a remnant of righteous people were saved and these were identified by *a mark upon their foreheads*. The mark of the beast in Revelation 13:16-18 is the Devil's deceptive *counterfeit* of this godly mark.

Albert Pike, Luciferian and Patriarch of American Scottish Rite Freemasonry, in his classic book *Morals and Dogma*, pages 503-504, writes: [The prophet Ezekiel, in the 4th verse of the 9th chapter, says: "And the Lord said unto him, Go through the midst of the city, through the midst of Jerusalem, and *mark the letter Tau* upon the foreheads of those that sigh and mourn for all the abominations that be done in the midst thereof."

So the Latin Vulgate, and the probably most ancient copies of the Septuagint translate the passage... It was a sacred symbol among the Druids. Divesting a tree of part of its branches, they left it in the shape of a *Tau* Cross, preserved it carefully, and consecrated it with solemn ceremonies. On the tree they cut deeply the word *THAU.*]

The King James Bible together with its underlying Received Text records *no* such *"Tau"* at all in the text. The *Tau* appears only in the corrupt Roman Catholic text underlying modern bibles. The *Clementine Vulgate (1592)* scribes, amazingly, have added the *Druid "THAU"* to their spurious Latin text in Ezekiel 9:4. The old Babylonian Devil has a pre-occupation with changing this particular key biblical text. Obviously he is addicted to suiting himself and his sun-god Tammuz, because he doesn't yet want to receive the mark of the LORD by faith in Jesus Christ into his forehead [temple].

Tertullian informs us the *Tau* was inscribed on the forehead of *every* person who had been admitted to the Mysteries of Mithros. In the Indian Mysteries, the *Tau* Cross, under the name of *Tikuk* was marked upon the body of the candidate. The *Tau* Cross is found on the stones in front of the Temple of Amunoth III, at Thebes, who reigned about the time the Israelites took possession of Canaan. At that time, it was the practice of all the Egyptian priests to carry it in their processions.

All of the planets known to the Ancients were distinguished by the Mystic Cross, in conjunction with the solar or lunar symbols; Saturn by a cross over a crescent, Jupiter by a cross under a crescent, Mars by a cross resting obliquely on a circle, Venus by a cross under a circle, and Mercury by a cross surmounted by a circle and that by a crescent. The logo of the *Prince of Wales Trust* incorporates the letter "C" for Charles, the symbol of a crescent. Above the crescent is a crown surmounted by the *Crux Ansata*. The 'crescent' of Islam is the "C" for Charles. Mounted atop the golden dome of the Dome of the Rock in Jerusalem, is a vertical shaft representing a cross. Upon this cross is mounted the crescent circle of Islam. It is this *precise* symbol in the form of the *Crux Ansata* that symbolized Pharaoh Ramesses II, and it is also now the symbol that is surmounted on the crown of the *Prince of Wales Trust!*

In more recent times, the *Crux Ansata* was adopted

by the popular satanic Rock Star *Prince* who appropriately used it as the mysterious 'unpronounceable symbol' of his name. In witchcraft, the *Tau* is the emblem of the phallus, Mercury and Hermes.

When Israel *first* struggled to possess the land of Canaan that God had unconditionally promised them *forever*, the *Crux Ansata* was at that time the principal symbol of the enemy of God's people. In the 'last days' heralding Jesus Christ's return, when all the great pagan Gentile nations of the world *finally* attempt to stop Israel from possessing the land God has promised them (even though, at present, Israel is still yet largely in a state of unbelief)—the *Crux Ansata*, or derivations of it, will once again symbolize the enemy's hate and rebellion.

Jesus warned in Luke 17:28: "...as it was in the days of *Lot*..."

While the whole world plays **"LOT-*T-O*"**—like the ancient Babylonians and Egyptians, who *reversed* the last two letters of just Lot's biblical name to make the *Crux Ansata*—the ignorant masses of the world, with six vertical strokes of the pen, repetitiously fill in their cards with the *Tau* symbol, and programme into their pagan minds the Devil's 666 number. [In the ancient Babylonian occult system, two straight bars (or lines) have always represented the *Tau* Cross and number 'six'].

The Tau cross of **'LOT-*T-O*'** in York Rite Freemasonry's Royal Arch degree represents the old Babylonian Devil himself, Hiram Abif (Tammuz). Hiram is the universal Masonic *Hero* and Christ-like figure. In truth, he is the Babylonian Antichrist.

Soon, like Tammuz or Pharaoh Ramesses II, a Pied Piper from Scotland, a Prince from Wales, a man from England, a counterfeit Lion of Judah, a counterfeit David, is coming to lead the youth of the world to hell. Cloaked in Christian robes and with a genealogy claiming to be the 'Messiah,' he is to be worshipped by the children of the world as their literal '*Holy Father.*' His badge of honour is the *triple Tau*, six hundred three score and six. He's the champion of every Girl Guide and Boy Scout. He is to be worshipped as their idol and saviour. Incarnated in the *Crux Ansata*, the Babylonian sun-god, he will finally win the hearts of his youthful audience, and be worshipped through the magical symbol surmounted upon the crowning glory of *The Prince of Wales' Trust.*

___Charles' Three Great Symbols:___ The *badge* of the Prince of Wales consists of *three ostrich feathers* enfiled by a gold coronet with a small scroll inscribed 'Ich dien' (I serve). Around the coronet are the *Maltese-Cross* and *fleur-de-lys* symbols. These three symbols have long been dominant in Roman Catholicism and European monarchy. They originate from Babylon and Egypt.

The *three feathers* and *fleur-de-lys* are ancient symbols that represent the Egyptian trinity, Osiris, Isis and Horus. Amun-Re, the great imperial sun-god of the _New_ *Kingdom* of Egypt was represented with two *large feathers* on his head during the period of Tuthmosis III.

Of all pagan symbols of the sun the *cross* is supreme. In particular, the *Maltese Cross* is the supreme symbol of pagan monarchy. In the British Museum in London there are two great Assyrian sculptures of antiquity.

The first, is Exibit #WA118805 in Room 26, the *Stela of Ashurnasirpal II (883-859 B.C.).* This stela was erected outside the Temple of Ninurta at Nimrod. In this amazing sculpture, the King is wearing a *Maltese*

Cross (the symbol of the sun) hanging from a necklace about his neck. He is holding a *Mace* upon which is a globe, the symbol of the earth and his divine authority. Above his right hand is a star, the planet Venus, symbolizing *Ishtar* (Easter), the great mother-earth goddess of Babylon.

The second, is Exibit #WA118892 in Room 27, The *Stela of Shamshi-Adad V (823-811 B.C.).* This stela comes from the Temple of Nabu at Nimrud. In this sculpture, the King is wearing a large *Maltese Cross* on his chest, the ancient symbol of the pagan Assyrian sun-god.

Long before the Christian Church ever was established, this Babylonian Cross was the symbol of the sun-god deity. Just like in Babylon it was used in Rome for crucifying criminals. This is the cross upon which our Lord Jesus was crucified. Throughout history, without exception, this cross has been the implacable enemy of the God of Israel, Jews and true born-again Christians. It is the blood-red cross of apostate Christianity. It is used in Freemasonry and just about every pagan witchcraft ritual in the world. The Pope wears it on his vestments. The Protestant Church uses it. Adolf Hitler used it. It is a universal symbol of military valour and it is the principal symbol of the British Crown.

The *Maltese Cross* is the symbol of the Knights Templar, the highest degree of York Rite American Freemasonry. This is the *only* degree that has the effrontery to offer prayers in Jesus' name, and in which the singing of the hymn *The Old Rugged Cross* is the central theme of its witchcraft ritual.

The *Maltese Cross* is the **Grand Symbol** of the **United States of America** and **Washington D.C.** It symbolizes the British Monarch's and Vatican's control of America.

Standing upon its hilltop home, like St. Peter's in Rome, is the American nation's greatest shrine, the Capitol. Deep within the building in an underground crypt lies the Capitol's Compass Foundation Stone. This is the zero point from which all of Washington's streets are numbered and lettered. This stone is the zero point and centre of the biggest *Maltese Cross* of any that dominate the great cities of the world.

The North arms of the *Maltese Cross* are New Jersey and Delaware Avenues. The South arms are Delaware and New Jersey Avenues. The East arms are Maryland and Pennsylvania Avenues. The West arms are Pennsylvania and Maryland Avenues. [On modern maps the cross is difficult to distinguish clearly, because Union Station obscures a large part of Delaware Avenue in the North East, and in the South West, a large part of Delaware Avenue is obscured by a labyrinth of motorways East of the National Historical Museum].

French Freemason, Peter Charles L'Enfant, designed the City of Washington, D.C. On his original plan of 1792, apart from other major occult symbols incorporated into the city, he gave the *Tiber Creek* a great deal of prominence. On his original plan he said, "The water of this *Creek* may be conveyed on the high ground where the Capitol stands and after watering that part of the city, may be destined *for other useful purposes*—The branch of the *Tiber* may be conveyed to the *President's House*." His words were prophetic.

In many respects, Washington D.C. is a modern replica of Rome. It is thus with the *"Spirit"of the"Tiber"* and the *"Cross"of "Babylon"* that this great American metropolis now stands. The city is divided up into hundreds of different squares. The 666th square is located at the bottom of South Capital Street. A street that incidentally traverses the *centre* of the Foundation Stone in the Capitol Building, the seat of power of the U.S. Government!

The time is not too far distant when these powerful symbols will come alive and return with a vengeance. The Empire will strike back, remove America's independence, and once again her people will become subjects of the *Maltese Cross* of the Roman Catholic/ Protestant British Monarch.

H.R.H. President Charles—Head of every 'Corporation' on Earth!

The American author, Joan Veon, in her brilliantly researched book, *Prince Charles—The Sustainable Prince—Who Will Rule The New World Order (1997)*, vividly outlines Charles' vast global interests. Her book reveals a man of exceptional intellect and immense power. He is *not* the character the media would have us believe!

In his capacity as President of the *Prince of Wales Business Leaders Forum*, H.R.H. Prince of Wales indirectly controls virtually *every* major corporation on earth. This includes all the world's environmental agencies, the United Nations, Club of Rome and World Bank. On pages 110-115 of her stunning book, Joan outlines the names of the corporations with their Chief Executive Officers, who were members of the PWBLF according to the Forum's 1990-1995 Report.

Her book reveals the Prince's influence and control over the world environmental movement, sustainable development, global governance, multinational-trans-national corporations and various U.N. agencies—plus much more. Her book is essential reading for all students of end-time world events.

The City of London Corporation

The City of London is an independent, private, sovereign state occupying approximately one square mile within the heart of the 610 square mile Greater London area. It is a separate, self-contained 'kingdom' in the centre of London. It even has its own police force. The Lord Mayor, who is elected once a year, is its ruler. Its resident population of about 5000 rises to about two million during the week when people surge in and out each day to work. The financial centre of Europe, it is often termed the 'wealthiest square mile on earth.' At its centre is the massive Bank of England. It is the control centre of virtually every major bank in the world. Linked with the Bank of England are a host of giant international banks, including the Rothschilds, that control directly or indirectly the finances of every nation on the globe. Through the Bank of England, the Rothschilds and their subsidiaries, the City privately owns and controls the U.S. Federal Reserve Banking Corporation, the Bank for International Settlements, the European Central Bank, the I.M.F. and World Bank and others. Even the Rockefeller interests in America are indirectly controlled by the Rothschilds in London.

Sir Ernest Cassel (nickname 'Windsor Cassel'), the German Jewish close friend and financial advisor of King Edward VII, was instrumental with Jacob Schiff, head of Kuhn, Loeb and Company, New York, with Paul Warburg, a partner in the firm, in establishing the United States Federal Reserve Board in 1913. The City of London *controls* Washington D.C.

Other countries are controlled through the Reserve Banking System as well. A leading part in establishing the present world "Reserve" banking system was played by Mr. Montagu Norman, Governor of the Bank of England. The City of London Corporation *rules* the financial world. Through its subsidiaries, via financing global privatizations, mergers and takeovers, it has become the "head office" of the *"Corporation of Earth."* The Queen is head of the Corporation and sometimes refers to it as *"The Firm."* While ostensibly the power of the Monarchy appears to be diminishing, as the Queen voluntarily gives the Commonwealth countries their independence and she works toward *abolishing* the sovereignty of Britain—her City of London Corporation is quietly taking over the world.

The City is not part of England and is not controlled by the British Parliament. It is ruled over by a Lord Mayor. The Lord Mayor is an extremely important person in the City. Many people believe he has more power than the Queen, but this is simply not true. Contrary to public opinion, the Queen *does not* have to ask his permission to enter the City. When the sovereign wishes to visit the City, the Lord Mayor goes up to the City boundary (marked by the griffin in the middle of Fleet Street) to *greet* her, not to grant her permission to enter the City. The sovereign halts just inside the City boundary, and there the Lord Mayor advances toward the royal coach, carrying the Pearl Sword of Elizabeth I, its point lowered in *submission.* He surrenders it with an expression of *loyalty* and it is returned to him with equal courtesy.

It is often said the Queen is just a "figurehead." This could not be further from the truth. The fact is, the British sovereign both *owns* and *rules* the City. To understand how this mysteriously occurs, one needs to study a little bit of British banking history. The Jews, who were always masters of banking and finance, were first brought to England by the Normans after the conquest of William the Conqueror in 1066. From this time, written credit agreements in the form of the 'Jewish Gage' called a 'shetar' or a 'starr' were first used in England. Many of these shetars are still preserved in ancient English documents. From around 1200, the Jews in England allowed credit agreements to be written in the Latin or Norman French language of the time. Hence the modern English word 'mortgage' originates from the Norman French period in London. In French, '*mort*' means 'death' and '*gage*' means 'bond.' [Undoubtedly, there is a time not too far distant when many people in the world who have *mort-gages* will understand the true and deeper meaning of the term!]

The Jews in Norman England were held in the exclusive domain of the King's personal control, living at his sufferance and according to his wishes. Edward the Confessor issued a statute that included a statement "Jews and all their chattels are the King's property." As chattels of the King, the Jews retained their own property at his pleasure. Jews could not have anything of their own, because whatever they acquired, they acquired not for themselves but for the King. They lived where the King permitted, and when they died, their property was vested in the King. The underlying reality was that the Jews were no more than the King's accounts receivable clerks. Jews were subject to periodic tithing whenever the King demanded them to turn over money that was held, ultimately, on his behalf. The King preserved the Jews and their investments as representing his own financial future. The Jews were able to finance excursions to continental Europe and fund the Crusades.

The King's Exchequer greatly benefited from the dealings of the Jews. At times they were allowed to accumulate immense wealth through their money-lending.

From the time of William the Conqueror (1066), the genius of the Jews and their skill as moneylenders was highly respected by the King. They contributed a huge amount of money to the Royal Treasury and were treated as a necessary evil by the monarch. However, as creditors they were hated by commoners and ordinary people.

Whenever there was a poor harvest that resulted in a severe downturn in the economy, farmers and merchants often defaulted on their debts. This inevitably resulted in an attempt by the Jews to seize their property. When this happened, invariably debtors tried to kill the Jews and destroy the loan records. During the Coronation of Richard I in 1189 there were riots against the Jews which culminated in the Massacre at York on Friday, March 16, 1190. Rather than suffer torture at the hands of their debtors, the Jews in York sought refuge atop Clifford's Tower in the Royal Castle where they all committed suicide. After the event, both creditor and debt records had been eradicated. When Richard I returned from the Crusades he was displeased by the attacks against his moneylenders. Since all debts and wealth created by the Jews ultimately reverted to him, he was extremely upset that the debt records had been destroyed. Understandably, he took action to ensure this would not happen again. By 1200, his concern prompted the establishment of Archae (Registry of Bonds) and the Exchequer of the Jews. Soon Archae were established in all English towns with sizable Jewish populations. The Registries consisted of Chirograph Chests and four Chirographers. The Chirograph Chests preserved the bonds of debt and deeds of acquittance, and the Archae preserved the Chirograph Chests for the King's Exchequer.

To this very day, _all_ mortgages, bonds, loans etc. throughout the world—whether they be to homeowners, farmers, big business corporations, city councils or governments—indirectly or directly—are "registered" under the jurisdiction of Jewish controlled banks domiciled in the City of London Corporation under the subordination of the British Sovereign.

[A more in-depth understanding of the original English Common Law Mortgage and the Jewish Shetar's effect on English Law as it survives today, and from which much of the above detail is taken, may be found in the _Georgetown Law Journal Vol.71: 1179-1983 pages 1179-1200]._

Events surrounding the massacre of Jews at York in 1190, were later memorialized by Jews who arrived in the New World in America. New York and York Rite American Freemasonry are named in recognition of the event. Will the Jews ever learn? The York Massacre of 1190 was repeated by Adolf Hitler during the Third Reich where he blamed the Jewish bankers for all of Germany's problems. Many believe the biggest loan default and banking crisis in world history is soon-coming. When it comes, events in York of 1190 and those of the Nazi Third Reich will pale into insignificance. This time, "New York" and the whole world financial system is at stake.

In a sense, we are all to blame. If the Gentiles spent more time in study rather than sitting at sports stadiums or in front of their televisions, they would not be so easily deceived. If the Jews followed God's laws in the Bible relating to finance, and didn't charge usurious interest rates and so on, they would not be so hated.

Britain was one of the later additions to the Roman Empire and was a province of Rome for nearly four centuries, from A.D.43 to 410. During this period of domination, the Romans built a wall around the City of London. Inside the City they constructed a temple to Mithras (the sun-god) and a temple to Diana (the mother-earth goddess). Today the remains of the Temple of Mithras may be seen located a short way down Queen Victoria Street. The Altar of the Temple of Diana is located off Gresham Street. Both Roman soldiers and London merchants worshipped these gods. Guildhall, or the Hall of the Corporation of the City of London, is sited directly across Wood Street in line with the Altar of the Temple of Diana. Now, the old Roman "walls" of the Roman City constitute the borders of the City of London Corporation. In essence, the City of London *Corporation* is the modern equivalent of the *Pomerium* (sacred area) of ancient Rome.[The Latin word '*Pomerium*' derives from the Latin '*post-moerium,*' which means '*behind the wall.*']

Guildhall is now used for the City's municipal meetings, the election of the Lord Mayor and Sheriffs, and for State banquets. At the far end of the hall is the Musician's Gallery, guarded at each end by the famous figures of the legendary giants, *Gog and Magog*. The ancestors of the present figures were made of wicker and were paraded in pageants, and their basket-work hands were used to present petitions. The present Gog and Magog are sombre creatures in green-brown war paint picked out in gold. They are over 9ft tall and weigh over 15cwt. At the restoration of the effigies of Gog and Magog at the Lord Mayor's Banquet at Guildhall on Friday, 9th November, 1951, Sir Winston Churchill during the course of his speech said; "It seems that they (i.e., Gog and Magog) represent none too badly the present state of world politics. World politics, like the history of Gog and Magog, are very confused and much disputed. Still, I think there is room for both of them. On the one side is Gog, and on the other side is Magog. Be careful, my Lord Mayor, when you put them back, to keep them from colliding with each other, for if that happens, both Gog and Magog would be smashed to pieces and we should all have to begin all over again—and begin from the bottom of the pit." (*The Times*, London, November 10, 1951, page 6) Many Christians believe the references to Gog and Magog in the Bible refer to a future invasion of Israel from the north. The prophesy is to have two fullfilments. In February, 1998, German Chancellor Helmut Kohl became the *first* European leader to be made a Freeman of the City of London Corporation at a special ceremony in *Guildhall*. Mr. Kohl was given this unique honour by the City for his outstanding contribution to the peaceful reunification of Germany, and his work in implementing the European Currency Union with the Single European Currency. (*International Express*, February 24, 1998, page 15).

In reference to Gog and Magog in Guildhall, the prophesy against Gog, the *chief prince* of Meshech and Tubal in Ezekiel 39:6 is very clear: "And I will send a *fire* on Magog, and among them that dwell carelessly *in the isles*: and they shall know that I am the LORD." The corporate 'Holding Company' of the British Sovereign is called the "*Club of the Isles*."

The Coat of Arms of the City of London includes a shield upon which is the *Cross of St. George* and a *red dagger*. The shield is supported by *two dragons* and is crowned by a *knight's helmet*. Underneath is the Latin motto: *'Domine dirige nos'*—'Oh, Lord, guide us.' When Prince Charles was invested Prince of Wales he was given *The Gold Ring—two dragons* clutching an amethyst. These are the *same two dragons* that are emblazoned on the Coat of Arms of the City of London Corporation.

We remember, the Cross of St. George is the Roman Catholic/apostate Protestant Church's symbol and representation of the old Babylonian sun-god incarnated in the King. It is appropriate therefore, that it is the *central* symbol of the final Gentile World King's *'Corporation of Earth.'* Upon the shield is a *double edged red dagger*. This dagger is a substitute of the double-edged dagger by which Ehud killed Eglon, the King of Moab, the arch-enemy of Israel. (Judges 3:12-31).

The centre of African witchcraft is a 14,178-foot-high mountain in Kenya called *Mount Elgon*. The name is surprisingly reminiscent of *Eglon*, King of Moab, mentioned in the Bible. The road to Mount Elgon is a segment of the *Aids Highway*, the Kinshasa Highway, the road that cuts Africa in half along which experts say the AIDS virus traveled during its first breakout. (*The Hotline*, by Richard Preston, page 295). Many occultists say the AIDS virus originated on Mount Elgon in the area of Kitum Cave, located 8000—9000 feet up the mountain on the *East* side. (Of course this is not correct, but is pure witchcraft. The real truth is that the AIDS virus originated in the laboratories of government agencies and drug companies contracted to the United Nations World Health Organization vaccination programme.)

In October, 1990, when Sir Laurens van der Post wrote the Foreword to Anne Baring and Jules Cashford's book, *The Myth of the Goddess,* he said: "But here at last is a work of immense pioneering significance... It is a great story that they have to tell and it is a timely story, because it is the loss of this feminine eventfulness which has led to the most urgent and dangerous problem of our time: the exploitation and also the rejection of our *Mother Earth,* our mother not only deprived of the great store of life it had prepared for us but increasingly being denied the chance to do more." Sir Laurens van der Post, a writer and explorer, and former political adviser to Prince Charles' favourite uncle, Lord Mountbatten, was the spiritual mentor and major single influence over Charles' life in his early years. Sir Laurens was knighted in 1980. He was the inspiration behind Prince Charles' establishment of the UK Wilderness Foundation, registered charity No. 277856, on February 28, 1979. At the Wilderness Foundation's launch, the Prince appointed Sir Laurens van der Post, Sir David Checketts, the Duke of Wellington and Mr. Edmund de Rothschild as trustees. From this arose the *4th World Wilderness Congress* held in Denver, Colorado, in 1987, that was promoted by Baron Edmond de Rothschild, that resulted in establishing the ***World Conservation Bank.***

In 1925, Carl Gustav Jung, the occult Swiss analytical psychologist, and Laurens van der Post separately visited *Mount Elgon* where they lived for several months with the Elgonyi tribe studying their myths, dreams and witchcraft. Some years later, they met and became close friends. In March, 1977, Prince Charles paid a secret visit to Africa, inspired by the ideas and witchcraft of Laurens van der Post and Carl Gustav Jung. He visited the Elgonyi tribe on Mount Elgon. There, (according to Laurens van der Post), he had 'a road to Damascus and blinding flash' experience. Later, before he left Africa he spent time in Ghana where he met Asantehene, King Otumfuo Opoku Ware II, and the Queen Mother, Nana Afuah Takyiwaa II. There, he sat on a throne while he was crowned *"Charles Naba Nampasa"*—which translated means, *"Charles who Helps Mankind."* (*The Prince and the Paranormal* by John Dale, page 12).

In the soon-coming global financial meltdown, all loans and mortgages in default throughout the world will be ingeniously repatriated to the King. The *World Conservation Bank*, established under the direction of the late Baron Edmond de Rothschild, in 1987, at the *4th World Wilderness Congress*, in Denver, Colorado, is the *'vehiculum deceptivus'* chosen to implement this seizure. George W. Hunt, an American Christian businessman who attended the Congress, over ten years ago, in his stupefying, highly informative video *The New World Bank, Religion and Rulers* succinctly revealed how this was all to be achieved. The world's wilderness areas designated as U.N. mandated World Heritage Parks and Biosphere Reserves are to be used as the collateral for the capital-base of the Bank and its new currency, the World Conservation Dollar. When the global financial system crashes bringing national currencies and banks down with it, the 'securitized' assets (people's home loans, mortgages and bonds etc.) and the debts of the collapsed banks throughout the world, are to be 'swapped' for new *World Conservation Bank* loans issued against the collateral of *mother-earth*. Interestingly, the "**C**" for Charles and world Conservation, is the "**C**" symbol for Charles on the "*euro*." The "=" two cross-bar on the "*euro*" are the ancient symbol of the *mother-earth goddess*.

Of course, this is a satanic dirty-trick. It may sound good creating loans to protect the *earth* in the name of world conservation. However, in reality, the world's wilderness areas have no 'earnings engine' and are valueless *dirt*. When Ehud killed *Eglon*, king of Moab, with his dagger, (that he had previously given the king as a present, and which now is emblazoned on the shield of the City of London Corporation in the name of the king of England), out of his belly came valueless *dirt*. (Judges 3:22) This is ultimately the *judgement* that is coming upon the king and his dirty 'Earth Corporation'—a brutal scene re-enacted at the end of *Gladiator!*

When the planned world economic crash comes, and the World Conservation Bank policies are implemented, this diabolically evil, ingenious, incredibly cunning transaction will transfer the entire assets of the *Earth* to the *Queen* (the incarnation of the mother-earth goddess)— and these assets will be held in *Trust* for Prince Charles—the coming World *King* (the physical incarnation of the Babylonian sun-god). During this chaotic process, all savings will be wiped out. Stock markets will crash. Gold and silver will become almost worthless. (James 5:1-3). The World Conservation bank will be used as the 'de-coupling mechanism' to transfer the assets of the collapsed banks of the world to the *Protestant* Monarch. In the deluded words of Baron Edmond de Rothschild, "It will involve a new Magna Carta. A second

Marshall Plan. A new World Currency System. The Bank must know no frontiers or boundaries. It is our only hope for the world." Under the direction of the Prince of Wales, the author of environmental care and protection, the hypocritical Gentile king and his ungodly Jewish vassals in the City of London Corporation—the World Bankers—the very people who are responsible for destroying the rain-forests in Brazil and forests of the world, now propose through their devilish policy of 'Sustainable Development' promoted by the World Conservation Bank, to preserve our ecology, bring peace to Mankind and save the world!

"MYSTERY, BABYLON THE GREAT, THE MOTHER OF HARLOTS AND ABOMINATIONS OF THE EARTH" of Revelation Chapter 17 apparently refers to the corrupt Roman Catholic Church and apostate Protestant Church. Revelation, Chapter 18, however, is a different matter. Revelation 18:1 commences, "And *after these things* I saw *another angel* come down from heaven, having *great power*; etc..."

The whole chapter is difficult to apply to Vatican City, but applies perfectly to the *City of London Corporation* with the pomp and pageantry of the apostate Protestant British Monarchy—a Monarchy that soon is to be *abolished*, then restituted, to allow its "Chief Executive Officer" to rule the world!

"...*I sit a queen*, and am no widow, and shall see no sorrow." (Rev.18:7)—"that great *city*, that was clothed in fine linen, and purple, and scarlet, and decked with gold, and *precious stones*, and *pearls*!"

"And every shipmaster and all the company in ships, and sailors, and as many as trade by sea"—"the voice of *harpers*, and *musicians*, and of *pipers*, and *trumpeters"*—(excerpts from Revelation 18).

"The **merchandise** of gold, and silver, and precious stones, and of pearls, and fine linen, and purple, and silk and scarlet, and all thyine wood, and all manner of vessels of ivory, and all manner of vessels of most precious wood, and of brass, and iron, and marble, and cinnamon, and odours, and ointments, and frankincense, and wine, and oil, and fine flour, and wheat, and beasts, and sheep, and horses, and chariots, and slaves, and *souls of men.* "(Rev.18:12-13) "...*for thy* **merchants** *were the great men of the earth*; for by thy sorceries were *all nations* deceived." (Rev.18:23). [Inside **Guildhall**, or the Hall of the Corporation of the City of London, hang *twelve great banners* representing *twelve great livery companies*—the Mercers, Grocers, Drapers, Fishmongers, Goldsmiths, skinners, Merchant Taylors, Haberdashers, Salters, Ironmongers, Vintners and Cloth-workers. There are 69 other companies. Each was originally formed as a kind of friendly society to look after its merchant members, and to fix wages and standards of workmanship. These banners now symbolize the *twelve great corporations,* with their many companies, under the wings of the *City of London Corporation,* that are taking over the world.] The Chief Executive Officers of these companies are surely the *"great* **merchants** *and men of the earth!"*

Britannia, the name of Britain is as old as Caesar. "Rule Britannia, Britannia rules the waves," the great Protestant nation that gave the world the Bible in the English language, "never, never, never shall be slaves," her pompous subjects sang before the Second World War. Her monarch, dressed in "fine linen, purple and scarlet, and decked with gold." With her "precious stones, and pearls," the *Crown Jewels* of the British Sovereign (which include many of the most precious jewels in the world), stored in the Tower of London in the *City of London Corporation*. Her Lord Mayor's sceptre of power, the Pearl Sword of Elizabeth, and so on. With her "*merchants* which were made rich by her"—"that great *City*, wherein were made rich all that had ships in the sea by reason of her costliness!"—"What *city* is like unto this great *city*!"—the ***City of London Corporation***!

Jesus said; *"For what shall it profit **a man**, if he shall gain the **whole world**, and lose his own soul?"* (Mark 8:36)

In chapter four, the author outlined how the propaganda film *Pocahontas* was used to seduce the American people. Captain John Smith portrayed the role of the 'World Hero.' Evil Governor Radcliff played the part of Governor George Bush (Jnr). Just past Bread Street, next to a church called *St. Mary-le-Bow,* rests an amazing memorial—the statue of *Captain John Smith,* first governor of Virginia, whose life was saved (in 1608) by the thirteen-year-old Red Indian princess, Pocahontas, who became the *first* American to visit England. Where is *St. Mary-le-Bow*?—in the **heart** of the ***City of London Corporation!***

A Hero arises from the sands of the Roman Colosseum. He is the World Champion and coming World King.

In his *right hand* he holds the ancient occult *Emerald tablet of Hermes*—the royal *'Sceptre with the Cross'*—the symbol of power of the British monarch. [the *emerald* is set in the centre of the cross, and the royal sceptre is always held in the British monarch's right hand, as is the *Emerald tablet of Hermes].*

Hermes—the mythological author of Freemasonry and of ancient and modern witchcraft—the pagan name for Cush, the son of Ham who begat Nimrod, the founder and first king of Babylon (Gen.10:1-10). In Egypt, the synonym for the 'son of Ham' was '*Her-mes.*' Hermes (or Cush) was the original prophet of idolatry, the ringleader behind the building of the *great city and tower of Babel* (now the '*City and Tower of London*'). As the pagan 'interpreter' of the gods he was the one who caused the language of men to be divided and was called the 'divider of the speeches of men.' Cush or Chaos, Bel (and the dragon), he was the 'god of confusion,' the 'Bel-athri' 'lord of the spies,' the angel and messenger of Jupiter. In the Eleusinian Mysteries at Athens, his secret doctrine was kept in the *stone* '*Book Petroma.*' Hermes Trismegistus' '*Book Pet-Rome,*' the book of the 'Grand Interpreter' became the apostatized '*Peter*,' the Roman Catholic Pope and spiritual leader of Rome. In Babylon, his name was 'Meni' from Hebrew 'Mene'— 'the numberer.' Westminster Abbey, the Collegiate Church of *St. Peter* and the Chapel of *St. Peter ad Vincula* (in the *Tower of London palace)* thus became the Protestant 'St. Peter' in London. "*MENE, MENE, TEKEL, UPHARSIN*" (Daniel 5:26)—the writing was on the wall of Bel-shaz-zar's palace—and so too, God hath "numbered" the days of the British Sovereign, the King and Queen of Mystery Babylon.

Finally—the crowning capstone of global apostasy— a *Pontifex (Pope) Maximus* of the apostate *Protestant Church!*

CHAPTER TEN

ENVIRONMENTIUS MAXIMUS: DESTROYER OF THE EARTH

The oldest of all alchemic formulae is the sacred *Emerald* **of** *Hermes*. Hermes was the founder of all Egyptian learning, co-inventor with Isis of writing—(and we might add, the world's telephones and computers). He was the founder of all arts and sciences and healing, the author of Freemasonry. The Scandinavians worshipped him under the name of Odin, the Teutons as Woden, the Orientals as Buddha, the Babylonians as Marduk. He had a sacred tree and a precious stone, an *emerald*. He was represented by a serpent, a globe with wings, the sun and moon and a dragon. He is the CHiram of modern Freemasonry—the Babylonian antichrist.

The green *'emerald'* of Hermes, *the '*<u>*gemstone*</u>*' of the New World Order,* is the counterfeit of the *'emerald'* of Judah, the fourth precious gemstone in Aaron's breastplate.

In Revelation 21:9, the walls of the New Jerusalem are garnished with all manner of precious stones. (Not all of these stones are the same as those in Aaron's breastplate—nor are they in the same order). One is, however, the fourth stone, an *emerald*. This is the *emerald* of Judah that gave us the Messiah, the real tree of life and the true Saviour of the world. This fourth stone in the wall of the New Jerusalem is a memorial and permanent reminder to Israel, that God will keep his promises and covenant with His people, those who believe through faith in Jesus Christ, forever.

In Revelation 4:3, there is a 'rainbow' round about the heavenly throne, like an *emerald*. In Revelation 10:1, a mighty angel came down from heaven with a 'rainbow' upon his head prophesying of 'two witnesses' (i.e., the 'two olive trees' mentioned in Revelation 11:4 and Zechariah 4).

These 'two witnesses' represent Jewish and Gentile Christian believers in the last days, who will be given power to preach and prophesy etc. for 1260 days (Rev.11). As the 'times of the Gentiles' draws to a close with the 'dawning of the new Millennium,' the *emerald* of Judah and these 'two olive trees' quickly become the global and indeed, the Devil's chief focus of attention.

The arch-enemy of these two olive trees and the true tree of life (Jesus Christ) is, of course, Satan. He too, like Jesus, claims to be the 'Saviour' of the earth, but in reality he is the Devil and the Destroyer. **While using the twin lies of the deceptive slogans *Environmental Care & Protection* and *Sustainable Development* he goes forth to destroy the earth.**

In the last days, true Jewish and Gentile believers come together to worship and praise their Lord. (In

Hebrew, 'Judah' means to 'praise' and 'emerald' means 'to shine') In recognition of this fact both Jew and Gentile come together in Israel's true 'olive tree' and 'tree of life,' the Lord has revealed the name of the *World King* and angel of the bottomless pit in <u>two</u> *languages* and in <u>two</u> *names* in Revelation 9:11.

In the Hebrew tongue his name is *'Abaddon'* which literally means *'a green plant.'* In the Greek tongue his name is *'Apollyon'* which literally means *'destroyer.'* His full name is therefore: *'<u>A Green Plant Destroyer.</u>'*

HRH, The Prince of Wales, the author of 'Sustainable Development' and the destruction of agriculture. The 'environmental' 'prince of darkness', a modern-day Hermes or Jupiter. The ecumenical prince from England, the coming 'World King.' The royal patron of the World Church. The Protestant St. George. The Evergreen Green One. His bride, the mother-earth goddess (all nations of the entire world)—**<u>both</u>** Catholic and Protestant (the modern Pharisees and Sadducees), with the 'elders of Israel' (the World Council of Churches) representing all the heathen religions of the world (the crowds of the Colosseum)....

The farmer/earth-worker who went into exile, and became a soldier/gladiator. The hero of the Colosseum, who slew evil Commodus, and then sacrificed himself for his people ...<u>Environmentius MAXIMUS—DESTROYER OF THE EARTH!</u>

CHAPTER ELEVEN

THE FIRES OF THE 'VOLCANALIA'

Two great pagan Roman feasts were held in August every year. The first was the second articulation of the *Vinalia*, Rome's greatest feast, consecrated to Jupiter—the supreme god of light and god of the vines—and was celebrated on August 19th. (We remember that the first articulation of the *Vinalia* on April 23rd was the counterfeit of the end of *Seven Days of Unleavened Bread* ending Jewish *Passover.*) Why then, the double articulation on the Roman calendar?

The *first articulation* of the *Vinalia* is Satan's grand attack against the Lord Jesus' *First Coming* where he ate the Passover with his disciples. The *second articulation* is an attack against his *Second Coming* when his feet shall stand on the Mount of Olives and he shall save his people Israel. Both these attacks are concentrated in one supreme pagan deity, Jupiter.

In Israel, August 19th signifies the end of the Olive Harvest. The month following is Israel's *Feast of*

Trumpets (symbolically, the Second Coming of Jesus Christ). When Jesus was sharing his 'Last Supper' with his disciples he said: "But I say unto you, I will not drink henceforth of this *'fruit of the vine,'* until that day when I drink it new with you in my Father's kingdom. And when they had sung an hymn, they went out into the Mount of Olives" (Matthew 26:29-30).

When Jesus, whose name literally means *Jehovah Saves,* comes again at his Second Coming, he will save his people from the attack of all nations of the world, who come against Christians to battle and who in a modern guise worship *Jupiter* and observe the *Vinalia*. At this time, Jesus' feet will once again stand on the Mount of Olives (Matthew 26:29-30).

The two greatest feasts of Israel that the Devil hates the most are *Passover* and *Feast of Trumpets.* Both articulations of the *Vinalia* are synchronized to these special Jewish feasts. Both are accompanied by a *'Holocaust.'* The *Vinalia* of April 23rd is accompanied by the *Fordicidia* on April 15th and the *Cerialia* on April 19th (attacking Passover). The second articulation of the *Vinalia* on August 19th is accompanied by the *'Volcanalia'* on August 23rd (attacking 'Trumpets' the following month).

Saint Bartholomew's Massacre of the genuine Christian Huguenots by the Roman Catholic Church was synchronized to these *very* dates. (St. Bartholomew Day— August 24th)—Our testimony comes from *Fox's Book of Martyrs.* May the reader carefully note the dates: "On *August 22nd*, 1572, commenced this diabolical act of sanguinary brutality. It was intended to destroy at one stroke the root of the Protestant tree. The king of France had artfully proposed a marriage, between his sister and the prince of Navarre, the captain and prince of the Protestants. This imprudent marriage was publicly celebrated at Paris, *August* 18th, by the cardinal of Bourbon, upon a high stage erected for the purpose. They dined in great pomp with the bishop, and supped with the king at Paris—*four days* later, the prince (Coligny) was shot—At last, at twelve o'clock at night, on the *eve of St Bartholomew*, the signal was given. Immediately all the houses of the Protestants were forced open at once—priests holding up a crucifix in one hand and a dagger in the other, ran to the chiefs of the murderers, and strongly exhorted them to spare neither relations nor friends. Persons of both sexes and conditions were indiscriminately murdered; the streets ringing with doleful cries, and flowing with blood; and the houses ***flaming with fire***, the dead too numerous to bury, of which the world was not worthy."

To this very day, the massacres on St. Bartholomew's day are painted on the royal saloon of the Vatican at Rome, with the following inscription: PONTIFEX, COLIGNY, COLIGNY NECEM PROBAT, i.e., 'The Pope approves of Coligny's death.' Pope Gregory struck a medal to commemorate the event (an original is in the British Museum).

The ***Volcanalia*** was the second great Roman feast in August. Linked to the *Vinalia*, it was consecrated to Vulcan, the pagan ***'god of fire.'*** The site of the cult, which consisted of an altar, was situated south-east of the Capitol (temple of Jupiter) of Rome and thus outside the pomerium (sacred area) of the great city. A temple to Vulcan was built near the Circus Flaminius. [In Washington D.C., the Capitol (temple of Jupiter) and Mall area comprises the pomerium].

Vulcan, (the opposite of Vesta who represented the 'eternal flame'—similar to the 'Olympic flame,' or fire *'in'* the city) embodied the destructive fire *'outside'* the city. Which is why his cult was *'outside'* the walls of Rome. Vulcan helped destroy the enemy's arms. [American readers will observe this is why the Pentagon, Arlington National Cemetery, and the George Washington National Memorial and Grand Temple of York Rite Freemasonry, among other militaristic shrines—are located *'outside the walls'* of the Capitol in Washington D.C.]

Every year 'on the other side of the Tiber' during the festival of the *Volcanalia* small live fish (*genus pisciculorum vivorum*) were tossed into the fire in honour of Vulcan *'instead of human souls'* (*pro animus humanis*: Festus) or 'in order to redeem themselves.'—'Jupiter demands a life, Numa offers a fish?'

To commemorate the burning of Rome under Nero at the end of the first century A.D., the emperor Domitian ordered altars built 'to prevent future fires.' Each year on the day of the *Volcanalia,* a reddish-brown calf and a boar were sacrificed to Vulcan. With the construction of these altars to Vulcan throughout Rome, simultaneously, came the completion of the Colosseum. These two infamous events: The *'burning of the fires'* to Vulcan, and the 'opening of the Colosseum,' with its sports, games and entertainment spectacles heralded what was soon to become horrendous persecutions. This all quickly manifested itself in the martyrs of the Colosseum.

The remaining followers of Christ who were not cruelly martyred, sought refuge in the underground labyrinth of passages under Rome in the catacombs. It is a remarkable fact, the symbol used most commonly on the graves of Christians in the catacombs was the *'fish'*—(in Greek, the word for 'fish' is 'ichthus'—the acronym of the first letters of 'Jesus Christ, Son of God, Saviour')—Quite a contrast to the pagan symbol of the *fish* of the *Volcanalia*.

It is an irrefutable fact, *"all"* of the pagan religions of the world are elaborately founded upon *'fire worship,'* the worship of the 'sun' and 'nature'— 'mother-earth.' When Israel stopped worshipping their true creator JEHOVAH, they sacrificed their children by burning them in the *fires of Moloch.* When the apostate Church stops worshipping her Creator, JESUS CHRIST, then she, too, will sacrifice her children to the 'god of fire.'

Early in the year 2000 came the release of the film *Gladiator.* Then, in July 2000, after 1500 years of dereliction, the infamous Colosseum was once again re-opened. Following these events, in late August, coinciding with the *"Volcanalia,"* Protestant Britain, under the auspices of *The Great Fire of London Museum*, plans to re-enact the *Great Fire of London* of 1666—by burning a giant replica of the city that gave the world the King James Bible. (The centre-piece of the model to be burnt, just happens to be a replica of the tower of St. Paul's Cathedral, one of the greatest Christian landmarks in London. A building that, coincidentally, houses The Chapel of the Modern Martyrs, which contains a book of all the known Church of England martyrs since 1850).

Then the following month, in September, are the Olympic Games, the symbols of which are of the two great pagan deities—the Olympic *'flaming torch'* of Zeus/Jupiter/Vulcan, and a golden medal of Victory, the old pagan mother-earth goddess. Uncharacteristically, for the first time in history, the year 2000 Olympic medal depicts the Roman Colosseum in place of the Greek stadium.

Are we living in the 21st century? Or are we living in pagan Rome in the first century A.D. under the reign of Domitian? It certainly looks like we are living in a similar era. Did August 2000, with the feast of the *'Volcanalia'*, with its commemorative 'fires' lit throughout the Roman state herald a time of great persecution soon to come? Could the 'fires of the *Volcanalia'* and the burning of Rome under Nero, with the entertainments of the Colosseum—like Hitler's burning of the Reichstag was followed by the Olympics—be blamed upon Jews and Christians?

Soon the whole world will be worshipping the sun-god fiery Dragon incarnated in the flesh with his mother-earth goddess, for the communication buttons on the world's telephones are now the symbols of these two pagan deities. [The symbol (*) is the symbol of the *'sun'* and the symbol (#) is the symbol of the *"mother-earth goddess" (womb).*

The (*) in the form of a five or six-pointed *star*, is the ancient pagan symbol of *Saturn*. Hislop in *The Two Babylons*, says Kronos or *Saturn* was worshipped as Bel, Ninos or Nimrod. He was 'The Horned one,' 'the Mighty one,' (Genesis 10:8). He was the *'Father of the gods.'* In Babylon, he was represented by the gigantic 'horned man-bull.' The Ishtar Gate's two 'horned man-bull statues' now reside in the British Museum in London. The same word in Assyria that signified a *bull*, signified also a *ruler* or *prince*. Hence the 'Horned bull' represented the deified Assyrian *monarch* and signified *'The Mighty Prince.'*

The (#) is the ancient symbol of the *'mother-earth goddess.'* (to be precise, it symbolizes the *'vagina'* and '*entrance to her womb.* ') The ancient statues of *Castor and Pollux* consisted of '*two upright pieces of wood, joined together by two cross-pieces.* ' (In primitive pagan symbolism, two posts and just one cross-bar are often shown. Sometimes the entrance to the mother-earth goddess's womb is simply represented and shown as an 'arch').

The **emerald-green** <u>**screen**</u> on the world's modern mobile telephones, is none other than the ***Emerald tablet of Hermes***—the ancient pagan "*god of writing and cunning*"—the *author* of Freemasonry and world witchcraft. Two outstanding pictures of Hermes' 'Emerald tablet' appear in the classic Masonic book of witchcraft, *The Secret Teachings of All Ages*, by Manly P. Hall, pages XXXVII and CLVII.

In the book of Acts, Paul's journey to Rome while he was a prisoner of Julius, the **Roman centurion,** is a picture of Hebrew (and Gentile) Christian believers in the end-time Church. After Paul was shipwrecked on Malta, he departed for his trial in Rome on a ship whose sign was *Castor and Pollux*. (Acts 28:11) When he arrived in Rome to give his defence before Caesar (…"ye shall be brought before governors and kings for my sake" Matt.10:18), he must have been amazed to see there before him, standing inside the Pomerium in the very heart of the Forum, the temples of *Castor and Pollux* where they reside to this day.

The reader may reasonably ask. "How can two *male* gods be representative of the *female* divinity?"—Simple. They were '*the protectors of the entrance of their earth-mother's womb.* ' In Babylon, we remember, the Ishtar Gate was protected by the two 'horned man-bull statues,' who represented Nimrod-Baal (now in the British

Museum). In Roman mythology, *Castor and Pollux*, sometimes called the Dioscuri (twins) were famed for their mutual affection; they were guardians of the State and Temple of the Earth. They protected the hearth, led the army in war and were the gods of navigation. In the pagan religions of the world, they are sometimes represented as two obelisks, or pillars in front of heathen temples (and churches). They have long held the symbolism of Gemini, the patron of *phallic* worship.

Castor and Pollux symbolized by 'two pillars' are the pagan counterfeit of the two pillars of the house of the LORD, *Jachin* (meaning *will establish*) and *Boaz* (meaning *strength*) (2 Chron.3:17) and mentioned in Galatians 2:9 and Revelation 3:12. Freemasonry, like all other pagan *phallic* religions, passionately hates these two particular pillars.

The word '*obelisk*' meaning '*Baal's shaft*,' is always used to represent the male divinity. A 'point within a circle' is the pagan symbol of the sun and the male sexual organ. At the base of most obelisks, including St. Peter's, are to be found the pagan symbols of the 'testes'—a word in Latin that means 'witnesses.' ('a testicle' literally means 'a small witness'). The obelisk in the middle of St. Peter's Square is so sited that at a given point in the year the shadow from the sun on the shaft enters the door (i.e., *vagina*) of St. Peter's Basilica (temple of mother-earth) and shines upon the altar whereupon the incarnation of the Babylonion *fire-god*, Pontifex (Pope) Maximus sits.

In Babylon, the temple of Ishtar, mother-earth, was protected by two man-headed bull statues, one on either side of the Ishtar gate. Ishtar was represented by a lion. The front entrance to St. Peter's is protected by two lions and two pillars. Thus St. Peter's is a pagan temple of mother-earth.

In Washington DC, this symbolism is reflected in the obelisk which is the Washington Monument. The Capitol (temple of Jupiter) building is also a 'temple of the earth.' On the Temple Mount in Jerusalem, the Dome of the Rock is the 'temple of the *sun-god*' and the al-Aqsa Mosque the temple of the *'moon-goddess' (temple of the earth)*.

In London, the principal obelisk to Baal is 'Cleopatra's Needle,' sited on the Thames Embankment. It came from Heliopolis (City of the Sun) in Egypt. The new logo of *BP* (British Petroleum), released around July 2000, one of the most powerful oil companies in the world, is 'Helios' the Greek god of the sun, the pagan source of light to both gods and men of the earth. The great Protestant 'temple of mother-earth,' Westminster Abbey, is also accompanied by a male obelisk. In more recent times, the male sexual organ, symbolizing Baal's shaft, has its place in most cities in the form of the Sky-Tower.

The six-pointed star, Chiun (Amos 5:25-26) and Remphan (Acts 7:43), on Israel's flag is the symbol of the *'sun-god.'* The two horizontal bars on the flag symbolize 'the twins,' the *'mother-earth goddess.'* When Israel repents and is converted, the two symbols on her flag will be removed—leaving a 'pure white flag'- the *badge* of faith in Jesus Christ, the 'pure white mark' that identified the *badgers' foreheads'*—of the *badgers' skins* that covered the tabernacle of the LORD in the wilderness.

The six-pointed star, containing a six, within a six, within a six. The hexagram composed of two equilateral

triangles is made with *six strokes of the pen*. The Nazi
Swastika is made with *six strokes of the pen*. In late
1938– early 1939, if Nazi doctors felt a baby should be
killed, three doctors each marked the letter **"X"** on the
form with *six strokes of the pen*. In the psychological
programming of the masses, Goebbels believed if a phrase
was repeated often enough, no matter how ridiculous,
people would ultimately believe it in the end. When the
whole world plays *"LOTTO,"* they fill-in their forms,
with *six vertical strokes of the pen*. These *six vertical
strokes* are the Universal Product Code and computer
bar-code symbol for *666—the star of Saturn—antichrist*,
the coming **World King.**

Osiris or Nimrod in Babylon was *Saturn*. The name
Saturn in Chaldee is pronounced *'Satur'* but, as every
Chaldee scholar knows, consists only of four letters—
'Stur.' This name in Chaldee contained exactly the
Apocalyptic number 666:

$$
\begin{aligned}
S &= 60 \\
T &= 400 \\
U &= 6 \\
\underline{R} &= \underline{200} \\
&= \underline{666}
\end{aligned}
$$

The original name for Rome was *Saturnalia. 'The
city of Saturn.'* Another name for the Babylonian star
of Saturn was Jupiter *(lightning)* or Vulcan (fire). Vulcan
was the god of fire, king of flame, and was the forger
of the 'thunderbolts' by which havoc was caused among
the enemies of the gods.

The August 2000 *'fires of the Volcanalia'* with
'lightning flashes' from Vulcan/Jupiter herald **The Mighty
Prince**, gladiator and *'fire-god'* of the new millennium
Roman arena—**HRH, Pontifex Maximus!**

CHAPTER TWELVE

AMERICA'S CHOSEN EMPEROR: PRESIDENT GEORGE W. BUSH

At the beginning of the film *Gladiator*, Commodus usurped the throne from his elderly father immediately after a bloody battle in a smoky, fire-*blackened forest*. That battle was a propaganda representation of the U.S. Presidential Election in the year 2000.

First, the forest fires of the *Volcanalia* lit across America, "Vulcan destroys the enemies arms," then afterwards comes the U. S. Election!

The world public has been manipulated to become very cynical of politicians. The trend is toward 'coalition governments' and for election results to get closer and closer because people don't know who to vote for. Now it is simply a question of voting for the better of two evils. Concerned voters are becoming very discouraged. Either of the prime two presidential candidates could have become president. Democrat Al Gore is a rabid environmentalist and New Ager. Republican George W. Bush (Jnr) follows in the footsteps of his Masonic father. Both are New World Order advocates and are supported by the ruling Establishment. Both are not that popular. This all meant that the Election was going to be *very close*. But did the elite know in advance of the outcome?

Because George Bush (Snr) and George Bush (Jnr) are so vividly portrayed in the film *Gladiator* in a father/son relationship alongside Marcus Aurelius and Commodus, it therefore seems obvious that George Bush (Jnr) was **CHOSEN** as the new president of the United States of America.

Like Commodus, the new president was not elected to his position "by the will of the people." He was not the people's choice, but was put there by his father.

The overriding issue at stake was not *"who"* would become president, but rather, *"for how long"* there will be a president! The very essence of the great American Constitution—the Bill of Rights—and the whole system of democratic government is now under mortal attack. This is what the U.S. Presidential Election in the year 2000 was all about. The old American constitutional form of government must soon be *abolished* to make way for the New World Order government and final world leader. Soon the American Senate will become like it was during the reign of Commodus—little more than a local town-council.

If just one word could describe Commodus's dictatorial appointment it would have to be 'mockery.' It was the custom for emperors to choose their successor. Mostly they chose someone whom they considered able and respected by the people. When Marcus Aurelius appointed his son Commodus to succeed him, he mocked the very essence of Roman democratic government. Commodus should not have been appointed emperor by his father. He should have been appointed by the vote and will of the people. The elderly emperor should have known better, because even from his youth his son had mocked every vestige of Roman authority. After he was *illegally* declared emperor, his mockery, sexual deviancy and decadence rapidly got worse.

When Commodus was declared emperor, his appointment stirred up a strong feeling of resentment, embarrassment and unparalleled injustice for the Roman public. Soon the new emperor became a laughing-stock and a target for derision. Soon his rule, or rather the complete lack of it, caused confusion and chaos in the Roman Republic. The financial and justice systems quickly collapsed. There was a famine. Finally his despotic rule (180-192 A.D.) led to a sort of 'interregnum'—an interval during which the Roman State had *no* normal ruler. Historians generally date the appointment of Commodus (180 A.D.) as the <u>*beginning*</u> of the 'Decline and Fall of the Roman Empire.'

Commodus's appointment was synonymous of the spawning decadence in Roman society at the time. The gutless senate was filled with elderly, unprincipled, evil men who were more interested in lining their own pockets than they were in serving the people they were supposed to represent. The apathetic public was engrossed more in sports and entertainment than in preserving an honest and free government. The senate was filled with widespread corruption.

In short, the despotic activities of evil Commodus have come alive again and are now being re-enacted by the American government.

If ever there was justification for God's judgement falling upon a nation, it is *now*, in the United States of America! [Indeed, the corruption pervading the U.S. Government is symptomatic of what's happening all around the world]

Now the great, ignominious question is: Will *George Bush (Jnr)*, the *"new PRESIDENT of the United States of America"*—The Roman leader <u>*Commodus*</u> of the modern world—call the Senate together, in a state of global emergency for a general assembly in the U.S. Capitol, the Temple of the Earth?

Very likely indeed—because the United States Capitol (temple of Jupiter) building is crowned by the Statue of Freedom, the '*mother-earth goddess*'—and is adorned with the frieze of '*Ceres,*' lining the Capitol Dome. This means that the United States Capitol is, in fact, also a '*temple of the goddess of the earth.*'

After all, *Commodus, the emperor,* who sent the world into chaos and lost the respect of the Roman people, must be challenged on the sands of the Middle East arena—be *killed*, and be heroically *succeeded* by the final New World Order Leader.

Pontifex *Maximus*, the Roman/soldier hero *Gladiator*, the British Emperor Constantine, the patron saint of merry England, of Russia and the Muslims alike. Saint George, the victorious Christian soldier/martyr who valiantly served in the army of Diocletian. The Evergreen green One. The Environmental Prince of Peace. The author of Sustainable Development. The star Saturn. The New Age Christ. The World Teacher. The Lord Maitreya. The Buddhist's fifth Buddha, the Moslem's Imam Mahdi, the Hindu's Krishna. The Great Physician. The Great

Mathematician and Architect of the Universe. The Egyptian Horus. The World Master. The Greek Zeus. The Roman Jupiter or Vulcan. God of fire, the sun-god. Marduk, the great red dragon. Nimrod, the saviour of the world. A man's man. A man of the earth. The great destroyer:

Will it really be *"a man"* from London, England—*Maximus*—who saves the world? It certainly looks like it!

May the LORD have mercy on us all!

CHAPTER THIRTEEN

WORLD WITCHCRAFT, THE RITUAL SACRIFICE OF PRINCESS DIANA, AND THE SATANIC CALENDAR

Since writing my book, *Gladiator,* many fellow Christians have indicated it would have been good if more could have been written about the inter-relationship between the old Babylonian/Roman feasts and modern world witchcraft. Of particular interest to many is how these old pagan feasts have been gradually merged into the Roman Catholic/Protestant Churches and how they now impact upon major world events. The reader may find the following addendum interesting.

In the film *Gladiator*, near the beginning, Maximus enters a portable make-up temple where he dedicates the <u>sacrifice</u> of his wife and son to the "Blessed Mother" (Mother-earth goddess—"Diana") and his "Father" (Jupiter). In full witchcraft ritual, surrounded by flickering candles and wafting incense, he dutifully consecrates his beloved wife and son to a statuette of his pagan deity. When he prays to his "Father" and "Blessed Mother," an image of his wife and son are superimposed over the Satanic altar.

Not long after this pagan ceremony is concluded, Maximus's wife and son are ritualistically sacrificed and murdered. This takes place in a sort of tunneled pathway lined by high trees surrounded by fire. Thus, in the film, Maximus's sacrificial death symbolized (*Osirus*), his wife's (*Isis*), and their son's (*Horus*). All this was a re-enactment of the murder and sacrificial deaths of Dodi Fayed (*Osirus*), Princess Diana (*Isis*) and her unborn son (*Horus*).

Was Princess Diana, representative of *Isis*, ritualistically *sacrificed?* Diana was murdered on 31st August (a mirror-image of 13th August)—the car they were in crashed into the 13th pillar—she was murdered on the ancient "Diana" Mother-earth goddess sacrificial site in Paris at the Place de l' Alma tunnel—and her Satanic younger brother, Charles (Earl Spencer), had her buried, contrary to her wishes, at Althorp, on an island, in the middle of a lake, accompanied by four black swans, surrounded by trees, with a shrine and a flame dedicated to her memory.

It has been claimed by an occultist that Diana's ritualistic death was a Satanic human *sacrifice* designed to consecrate the period around the year 2000, with the birth of the New Millennium—to Satan! After Diana was taken from the tunnel, some of her blood, her foetus and other body parts would have been taken and distributed to be eaten by high level members of the Illuminati. But should we believe an occultist?

Since these claims relate to H.R.H. Prince of Wales, Pontifex Maximus, the possible future heir and 'Defender of the Faith'of the *Protestant* Church, or coming *World Church*, it's appropriate that we consider these claims in the light of the Bible.

Human Sacrifice in the Bible

In the Old Testament, when the *children of Israel* and the *children of Judah* apostatized, their *kings*, their *princes*, their *priests*, their *prophets* turned back from worshipping the lord God and set their abominations in the *house of the LORD.* When they did this, they "caused their sons and daughters to pass through the fire to *Molech* (Jeremiah 32: 26-35).

Is not this, now, *precisely* what is happening to the "*children of the Catholic*" and "*children of the Protestant*" Church?

"Because they have forsaken me, and have estranged this place, and have burned incense in it unto other gods, whom neither they nor their fathers have known, nor the kings of Judah, *and have filled this place with the blood of innocents*; They have built also the high places of Baal, to burn their sons with fire for burnt offerings unto Baal, which I commanded not, nor spake it, neither came it into my mind...*And I will cause them to eat the flesh of their sons and the flesh of their daughters*..." (Jeremiah 19:4-9).

"And I said, Hear, I pray you, O heads of Jacob, and ye princes of the house of Israel; Is it not for you to know judgment? Who hate the good, and love the evil; *who pluck off their skin from off them, and their flesh from off their bones; Who also eat the flesh of my people, and flay their skin from off them; and they break their bones, and chop them in pieces, as for the pot, and as flesh within the caldron.*" (Micah 3:2-3)

The Jerusalem Chamber, in *Westminster Abbey*, was the principal meeting place used by the translators of the King James Bible. This is the *house of the LORD* that gave the Protestant world her freedoms, the English language and the English Bible. But regrettably, like Israel—the rulers of Britain apostatized—they turned their backs on the LORD—they sacrificed to Baal—they set their abominations in the house of the LORD. "Their *kings*, their *princes*, their *priests* and their *prophets* caused their sons and their daughters to pass through the fire to *Molech*."

"And I saw *the woman drunken with the blood of the saints*, and with the blood of the martyrs of Jesus..." (Revelation 17:6)

"...And *the woman which thou sawest is that **great city***, which reigneth over the kings of the earth." (Revelation 17:16-18)

"...*I sit a **queen***, and am no widow, and shall see no sorrow. Therefore shall her plagues come in one day, death, and mourning, and famine; *and she shall utterly be burned with fire*: for strong is the Lord God who judgeth her." (Revelation 18:7-8). The start, "*Animal Disease*" in Britain.

"That **great city**," the ***City of London Corporation***, "which reigneth over the kings of the earth"—Her apostate *Protestant* sovereign, "***I sit a queen***"—*drinking human blood and eating human flesh* consecrated to Baal, in Westminster Abbey, the birthplace of the King James Bible—"and have burned incense in it unto other gods, whom neither they nor their fathers have known. This, now, reflects the pathetic state of the apostate *Protestant* Church! Indeed, what now is being done in secret behind closed doors, may soon be done openly, and become the "norm" in the final, abominable World Church! ***The Catholic Pope—a counterfeit of 'God the Father,' the Protestant Prince—a counterfeit of 'God the Son.'***

Jesus said to his followers, "Whoso eateth my flesh, and drinketh my blood, hath eternal life; and I will raise him up in the last day." (John 6:54)

Based upon these very words, he instituted the "Lord's supper" (Matthew 26:26-29), which was faithfully celebrated by the early Church. Then the Church of the Dark Ages perverted and changed it into the Babylonian "Mass." The Roman Catholic Church became *drunken with the blood of the saints.*

The great Protestant Reformation broke the yoke of Rome. The "Lord's supper" was re-instituted by the Protestant Church. But alas, like her Babylonian mother before her, she apostatized. Her apostasy was greater, for never before had so many in the world come to know the Truth. In her final act of rebellion, she worshipped Baal. She returned to Rome and Babylon, and she too *became drunken with the blood of the saints*!

Hislop in *Two Babylons*, pages 231-232, writes: It will be observed, however, that the *Great Red Dragon*, or Great Fiery Serpent, is represented as standing before the Woman with the crown of twelve stars, that is, the true Church of God, *"To devour her child as soon as it should be born."* Now, this is in exact accordance with the character of the Great Head of the system of fire-worship. Nimrod, as a representative of the devouring fire to which human victims, and especially children, were offered in sacrifice, was regarded as the great child-devourer—as the representative of *Moloch* or *Baal*, infants were the most acceptable offerings at his altar—Hence, the priests of Nimrod or Baal were necessarily required to eat of the human sacrifices—hence, "Cahna-Bal," the "Priest of Baal"—a devourer of human flesh.

It is appropriate, therefore, and entirely consistent with scripture, that the Hero-Gladiator and (coming) champion of the apostate World Church, conducts himself in this manner. It is proper that the pinnacle of global apostasy be headed be a man—Antichrist—a reincarnation of Nimrod—who, as the World High Priest of Baal, *drinks human blood and eats the flesh of children in Westminster Abbey*, the house of the LORD that gave the free world the mighty King James Bible. Further, it is appropriate also, that he "shape-shifts" into a "reptilian"—the Great Red Dragon—the symbol of His Royal Highness—the Prince of Wales! The hero *Gladiator* of the Roman Colosseum.

The following is a brief synopsis of *"Satan's Timetable"* stamped upon world events. The Devil is very <u>precise</u> you know? Hopefully these facts may reveal a few home truths.

The Satanic Calendar

It is important to remember, at the time of Moses, leading up to *Passover* and the salvation of Israel, Pharaoh's wise men and magicians in Egypt had *miraculous* powers. They *counterfeited* many of Aaron's miracles, yet the Word of God still prevailed. (Exodus 7). In Babylon, King Neb-u-chad-nez-zar's wise men were the

ASTROLOGERS. They were very wise men indeed, yet their knowledge and power could not compare to Daniel's. Both Moses and Daniel were servants of the God of Israel. They and their people all suffered persecution and tribulation. Yet God miraculously delivered them. As we near the time of *great tribulation* the scriptures have prophesied is soon to come (Matt. 24:21), there is to be a global re-enactment of the events of Moses and Pharaoh, Neb-u-chad-nez-zar and Daniel. Once again, Antichrist and his *Astrologers* are the arch-enemy of Israel, Jesus Christ (Passover) and genuine Christians (servants of God). Once again, God will miraculously deliver his people.

The more one reflects upon the apostasy and hypocrisy of the Protestant Church, with its manifestation in nominally Christian homes, the more one realizes the *root* of the problem has started with the "innocent" Christmas Tree in the living-room (symbol of Tammuz, the Sun-god) and the "innocent" child's Easter-egg at Easter-time (symbol associated with Ishtar, the Moon-goddess). These two Babylonian days, Christmas and Easter, are the greatest feasts of the Devil. There is no instruction in the Bible to celebrate them. Yet the great mass of the Christian Church, contrary to the clear teachings in the Bible, still persists in observing them. The failure of the Church in rooting out these pagan practices is the *single-most* important cause of her downfall. By neglecting to eliminate these great pagan feasts from her liturgy, her sons and daughters have either expanded the observance of astrology still further in the Church—or they have repudiated her hypocritical teachings altogether. It is time all genuine Christians took a firm and uncompromising stand on this issue.

The modern major pagan "sun" festivals like Christmas (Sol Invictus), Yule and Midsummer's Eve (around the summer and winter solstices), the vernal and autumnal equinoxes and the common "sun-signs" of astrology now used so widely throughout the world form the basis of modern witchcraft—a religion that worships "creation" rather than the "Creator."

Witches have eight major festivals throughout the year. One at both solstices and equinoxes, and one at four other times during the year: February—announcing Spring, April—heralding Summer, August—welcoming Autumn (Harvest), and October awaiting Winter. The major witchcraft festival is October 31 or Halloween. In this book, I have explained how the original Babylonian/Roman feasts are a counterfeit of the genuine Feasts of Israel—these old pagan rituals are the "purest" Satanic feasts of all. Not all the modern equivalents are the same as the originals, so we will not concentrate on them. The ones we will look at more closely will be the ones associated with Ishtar or Diana, the Mother-earth goddess and goddess of the **Moon.**

Ultimately, the Moon-goddess (Mother-earth) is the deity worshipped by the "mother of harlots and abominations of the earth." She is the deity of the "woman drunken with the blood of the saints" worshipped by the final World Church.

Ex-Satanists and now born-again Christians, William and Sharon Schnoebelen, in their compelling book, *Lucifer Dethroned* (published by Chick Publications), pages 329-333, write:

"Additionally, common to both witches and Satanists are the **lunar feasts**—26 in a year. These are called Esbats, and are celebrated on each *dark moon* and each _full moon._ Usually, black (i.e. evil) magic is done near or on the dark of the moon and white magic (healing, spells for finances, jobs, fertility) is done near or on the full moon."

"**The 13<u>th</u> and 31<u>st</u> day (if one) of the month:** Also Friday the 13th. Magic performed, but not necessarily physically dangerous."

We will now apply this knowledge to Satan's "Moon-goddess calendar" of modern events. The first subject we will deal with will be Arizona Wilder's testimony involving Charles and Diana.

✦ Special Note: All Moon phases, lunar and solar eclipse dates are taken from _The American Ephemeris for the 20th Century 1900 to 2000 at Midnight - Revised Fifth Edition_ - (Revised with Jet Propulsion Laboratory positions) by Neil F. Michelsen. (Most astrologers consider this _ephemeris_ is the most accurate).

Charles and Diana

Here is a brief summary of the key dates and events in the tragic life of Lady Diana—a Princess who was chosen _before birth_ to be Satanically _sacrificed_ as the "Moon-goddess" of the apostate Christian Church!

✦ July 1, 1961 (Full Moon, June 28)—Lady Diana born.
✦ July 29, 1981 (New Moon/Solar Eclipse, July 31)— Charles marries Diana.
✦ June 21, 1982 (New Moon/Solar Eclipse, June 21)— Prince William born.

✦ June 15th, 1992 (Full Moon/Lunar Eclipse, June 15)—
Andrew Morton's book *Diana: Her True Story*
released and drives Diana to attempt suicide.

✦ December 9, 1992 (Full Moon/Lunar Eclipse,
December 9)—British P.M. John Major announces
to Parliament that Charles and Diana are separating.

✦ August 28, 1996 (Full Moon, August 28)—Final
decree of divorce issued.

✦ August 31, 1997 (New Moon/Solar Eclipse, September
1)—Diana *sacrificed* on the Moon-goddess mirror-
image day of the *Ides of Jupiter* (August 13). (In
ancient Rome, her cult fell on August 13th).

Yves Bonnefoy, in *Roman & European Mythologies*,
pages 71 and 125, states: The etymology of Diana's
name is transparent: it is formed on the adjective *dius*
("luminous"); the neuter *dium* designates "the luminous
sky." Diana means "the luminous one" and therefore
comes from the same root *diu* - as Jupiter: she dispenses
nocturnal light, alternating with Jupiter, the god of day.
Cicero (*De Natura Deorum, 2.27.69*) gave a precise
definition of her name: "Diana is associated, it is thought,
with the _Moon_...she is called Diana because at night
she makes the day (*dium*)." The anniversary of her cult
falls on _13 August, the ides_, which formerly coincided
with the day of midsummer. It is therefore no accident
that the *ides* designated both _the anniversary of the temple_
of Diana on the Arventine _(13 August)_ and the anniversary
of the temple of Jupiter on the Capitol (13 September).
There is also the rite: even in Ovid's time (*Fasti, 3.270*)
women carried torches from Rome to Aricia, "carrying
the light" (*Propertius, 2.32. 9-10*) to the goddess. Diana
was originally worshipped in the sacred woods of this

Latin city—her cult was moved to the Arventine in Rome—tradition dates this transfer at the time of Servius Tullius, but it is more likely it took place in the *fifth century B.C.*—Diana became the protectress of slaves: the anniversary of her temple on the Arventine is called *Dies Servorum*, "the day of slaves."—Essentially she was the *protectress of feminine life.* Tradition localized this cult in Aricia, near Lake Nemi, which was called the *Speculum Dianae* (Diana's mirror). At Aricia, as in the case of Jupiter Latiaris of Mount Alban, a sacred grove preceded the *shrine* dedicated to Diana.

The account in Acts chapter 19, of Paul's experience in Ephesus with Demetrius, who made silver *shrines* for *Diana*, is a "picture" of the paganism in the end-time Church— *"Whom all Asia and the world worshippeth"* (Acts19:27)— *"what man is there that knoweth not how the city of the Ephesians is a worshipper of the great goddess Diana, and of the image which fell down from Jupiter?"* (Acts19:35).

Masonic author, Albert Pike, in *Morals and Dogma*, page 470, writes, "Diana of Ephesus, **the Moon,** wore the image of a *crab* on her bosom, because in that sign was the moon's domicile."

After nearly two thousand years of the Church being founded at Ephesus, a "Great is Diana of the Ephesians" was born to the world Church, on July 1, 1961, in the astrological *sign* of *Cancer* the Crab, ruled by the Moon. She was worshipped by the women of the world as the patron of motherhood, the *"protectress of feminine life"*—the essence of compassion, sponaneity and warmth, *"the protectress of slaves,"* the champion of selfless humanity—an icon of the modern woman—women deeply empathized with Diana—hero of the starving millions, Aids victims, the suffering, and the less than fortunate—she touched the hearts of millions. Like Diana of Aricia, near Lake Nemi, her cult was *"Speculum Dianae,"* (Diana's mirror)—she was sacrificed on August 31st, the *"Speculum Dianae"* of August 13th, the anniversary of her cult in Rome, the ides of *Jupiter*. She was buried with the *rosary beads* that had been given her by the late Mother Teresa—at Althorp, a modern "Lake Nemi," in a grove on an island surrounded by sacred woods—she had a Roman shrine, with a cross on top, dedicated to her memory.

Women carried torches from Rome to Aricia, "carrying the light"—Elton John sang his rewritten version of "Candle in the Wind," his old elegy to Marilyn Monroe, in tribute to Diana. In Westminster Abbey, the house of the Lord, the birth-place of the King James Bible, 1900 of some of the world's most famous celebrities honoured the "People's Princess." Lady Hillary Rodham Clinton, Steven Spielberg, Henry Kissinger, Tony Blair, members of the European royal families etc. The service bidding, said by the Dean of Westminster, the Very Rev Dr Wesley Carr, was followed By Gustav Holst's **Jupiter**, sung to the hymn *I vow to thee my country*. After the hymn *The King of Love my Shepherd Is*, Tony Blair read 1 Corinthians chapter **13** from a New Age Bible—"Diana" and "Jupiter" of the apostate *Protestant* Church!

Why was Diana sacrificed and murdered?

She had to be *sacrificed*, as the Moon-goddess, to create an *"emotional vacuum"* in the hearts and minds of the *women* of the world, to prepare them for the ultimate worship of the rising Sun-god (Horus), the "god of the day," Jupiter, her former husband, H.R.H. Maximus—the coming Champion Gladiator of the World Colosseum—the Great Red Dragon.

The Roman Catholic Rosary

Like Freemasonry, Roman Catholicism is a subtle form of *Astrology*. The number of beads on a Catholic Rosary is 54. This number is representative of the number of weeks in the leap year of the <u>Lunar</u> Calendar. Thus, the *Rosary* is an astral 'thought director" or *Astrologer's Prayer Necklace* from Babylon. From the top 54 beads of the Rosary hang another 5 more beads attached by a Virgin Mary medallion. At the bottom is usually a crucifix. The 5 beads in the necklace, (similar to Freemasonry's five degrees of The Eastern Star), represent the Satanic Pentagram. The Virgin Mary is the 'Christianized' form of the Babylonian *Moon-goddess*. The crucifix is a representation of the Babylonian *Sun-god*. This is why Diana was buried with Mother Teresa's "*rosary.*"

The Protestant Rosary

The corrupt *Revised English Bible,* that has now replaced the original *King James Bible,* that rests on the Great Lectern in Westminster Abbey, has on its cover a brazen picture of the cross of the Babylonian Sun-god around which are the 54 fruits of the *Moon-goddess's* lunar calendar or rosary! Now, suspended from the ceilings of Westminster Abbey are *eight* giant chandeliers (we remember, witches have *eight* major festivals throughout the year). Each chandelier contains exactly *540 pieces* of crystal and is shaped like a fish. Ostensibly the symbol of St Peter, in reality the fish-god Dagon. It is a "miracle" God's Word, the King James Bible, ever was translated from this pagan Moon-goddess temple!

Fatima Apparitions

The Virgin Mary (devil Mother-earth/Moon goddess), supposedly gave her miraculous heavenly message of peace to three shepherd children at Fatima in Portugal in 1917. Fatima just happens to be Muhammad's favourite daughter—the Moslem Mother-earth/Moon-goddess. The devil-goddess, "Our Lady," appeared to the children through a number of miraculous apparitions. These were on May 13, June 13, July 13, August 13 and 15, September 13 and October 13, 1917. Jesuit scientist Pio Sciatizzi described the October 13 apparition as "*The Miracle of the Sun*." "So that all the world may believe," over 70,000 present at Fatima "saw the sun dance in the sky and then plunge zig-zaggedly earthwards like a monstrous fireball."

Who is "*The Miracle of the Sun*?"—*JUPITER!* In Rome, we remember, the two principal festivals in his honour were the *Vinalia* which were celebrated on August 19 (the consecration of grapes) and on April 23 (the offering of wine). Apart from these two prime dates, he was also honoured on the "ides" of each month, which fell on the 13th of most months excepting March, May, July, and October when they fell on the 15th. On the "ides" of Jupiter, each month, a lamb was sacrificed and offered (as a monthly reminder of their hate of Jewish *Passover*). Thus, the apparitions of the Virgin Mary at Fatima are the Jesuit equivalent of the "*IDES OF JUPITER.*"

Inauguration of U.S. Presidents

In ancient Rome, the priests of Jupiter were given various names. Their names reflected their responsibilities.

The diviners were called "*Divinatio*," the official interpreters of Jupiter were "*Augurs*," and the official experts in the examination of portents and lightning flashes were called "*Hauspices*." This is why all U.S. Presidents are "*inaugurated*" into office under the seal of the American "eagle"—the ancient symbol of Jupiter.

In the Roman Catholic Church, *Jesuit priests* are the modern equivalent of the old Roman "*Hauspices*." In the Protestant Church, men like Dr. Billy Graham and Freemason, Dr. Norman Vincent Peale, are the modern equivalents of the "*Divinatios*" and old Roman "*Augurs*." Men like Dr. Billy Graham are the Protestant Church's "*Divinatios*" that tell lies and give *inaugural prayers* at the Capitol (temple of Jupiter).

Starting with Richard Nixon, who was inaugurated on January 20th, 1969 (New Moon January 18), with the exception of Gerald Ford, who was inaugurated on August 9, 1974 (because of Nixon's impeachment), *all subsequent U.S. Presidents have been inaugurated in synchronization with Satanic feast days*.

[Jimmy Carter: January 20, 1977 (New Moon January 19), Ronald Reagan: January 20, 1981 (Full Moon/Lunar Eclipse January 20), George Bush: January 20, 1989 (Full Moon January 21), Bill Clinton: January 20, 1993 (New Moon January 22), and January 20, 1997 (Full Moon January 23), George W. Bush (Jnr): January 20, 2001 (New Moon January 24)].

With the inauguration of George W. Bush on January 20, 2001, the witchcraft feast days are getting out of kilter with the appointment of the president. George W. Bush may be the last U. S. president.

Billy Graham: Evil Pretender and Colosseum Prophet

The "*subtlety and deception*" of the Roman Catholic Church's "Christianization" of the old Babylonian/Roman religion is only to be *exceeded* by that of the apostate *Protestant Church*.

A large amount has been written about the "abominations" of the Roman Catholic Church, but relatively little has been focussed on the *Protestant Church*. It is about time we focussed on some of the Protestant Church's abominations.

No greater evangelist and prophet, in modern times, can exceed the celebrity status of Protestant Dr Billy Graham.(Technically, Baptists are not Protestants) Accordingly, his ministry will be used as an example.

Conversion: From the time of Billy Graham's claimed "conversion," this author has observed the majority of his major experiences and Crusades have been "*synchronized to major Satanic Feasts and phases of the Moon.*" In his autobiography, *Just as I Am*, page 23, he says: "God saved me, and my eyes were opened, and old things passed away, and all things became new. I will never forget the *moonlit night.*"

Marriage: [We remember, the Protestant Moon-goddess, Princess Diana, was murdered and sacrificed on August 31, the *Speculum Dianae*, the mirror-image of the anniversary of her cult on August 13 on the "*Ides of Jupiter.*"] In Billy Graham's autobiography, *Just as I Am*, page 79, he says: "We were married there in *August*, on the *night* of *Friday the thirteenth*, with the *full moon* in the sky."

Dear reader, do you realize what the full implications of these disturbing facts mean? Surely there is not a genuine Christian man or woman in the world who would elect to be married on a *full moon*, *at night*, especially on *Friday 13th*. To this very day, in New Zealand, where this author resides, it is "*illegal*" to be married at night. What is even more disturbing is the fact that in 1943 there was only *one Friday* that occurred on the 13th of any month of the year—yet Billy Graham chose this *precise* day for his marriage. [The actual date of the full moon was on August 15, 1943. Incredibly, it was also a Lunar Eclipse].

Bel-te-shaz-zar or *"Bel-shaz-zar:"* In the book of Daniel, the king of Babylon, Neb-u-chad-nez-zar, made a sharp distinction between the Babylonian name he gave the *servant of God*, Daniel (*Bel-te-shaz-zar*), and that of his own pagan son (*Bel-shaz-zar*). It is often said, "a dog is a man's best friend." In Billy Graham's autobiography, *Just as I Am*, page 296, is a photo of Billy with his pet Great Pyrenes dog, *Bel-shaz-zar*, named after the king of Babylon's pagan son. (Hislop in *Two Babylons* says "Bel" is just another name for "Baal").

When stories came out criticizing Nancy Reagan's policy of consulting an astrologer on family and *national issues* after the assassination attempt on her husband, Billy said to her: "Nancy, surely you didn't really look into astrology, especially for something as important as *the dates when the cabinet should meet*." (*Just As I Am*, page 537)—This is a little bit like the pot calling the kettle black! What hypocrisy! Billy Graham has himself followed the cult of *astrology* from the date of his 'claimed' conversion!

Global Mission '95: In his autobiography, page 639, Billy Graham writes about his massive Crusade which transmitted his meetings via satellite to venues in 185 countries and territories throughout the world. He believes this Crusade may have been the most expensive single evangelistic outreach in the history of the Church. Millions upon millions of people watched these powerful programs that were translated into 48 languages.

Throughout the three individual night meetings of the Crusade, held on March 16th, 17th and 18th, Billy Graham specifically referred to the *full moon* in his address on *every night*. The middle night, March 17, 1995, of this Satanic Crusade, (where Billy sent his Roman Catholic "converts" <u>back</u> to the former vomit of the Roman Catholic Church, from which they originally came)—was appropriately, the *exact* night of the *full moon*.

Festival in the Park: Billy Graham's grand equivalent of Prince Charles' *'Party in the Park,'* called *Festival in the Park* or *Festival 96*, was planned to be held in Auckland, New Zealand, on Sunday, February 18, 1996 (New Moon February 18). Because of bad health, his trip had to be cancelled. The only difference between Prince Charles' *'Party in the Park'* rock concerts and Billy Graham's *'Festival in the Park,'* is that one has "secular" Satanic rock musicians and the other, "Christian" Satanic rock musicians." The Devil is the <u>same</u>.

<u>*Hitler and Billy Graham's Crusades:*</u> Hitler and the Nazis used astrology to set the timing of their mass-rallies. Just as women are naturally more easily seduced at certain times of the year, month and day, so he cunningly structured the timing of his speeches to deceive the German people. At his rallies, he imagined he was speaking to a *woman*. [Generally speaking, modern psychological warfare experts in Hollywood and the major

TV networks now call these times "prime-time television."]

In his autobiography, page 6, Billy Graham reveals, "I was *particularly fascinated* by the oratorical style of speeches shouted in an almost hypnotic voice by a man in Germany named _Adolf Hitler_."

In his autobiography, page 163, he says, "It was Willis, in his preliminary work in Columbia, who urged us to drop the word *Campaign* in favor of *Crusade*. The word *Campaign*, Willis pointed out, had been used for many years by evangelists, and was associated in the public mind with _outmoded_ (or even sensationalist) ways of doing things. A new word was needed, he felt, and we agreed on *Crusade*." Billy continues, "This was years before Vatican II's openness to Protestants, but we were concerned to let the Catholic bishops see that _my goal was not to get people to leave their church_; rather, I wanted them to commit their lives to Christ." ...Hasn't Billy read Rev. 18:4?

Billy forgot to mention, the reason why genuine Christian evangelists previously had shunned using the word "*Crusade*" in their ministries, was that the term previously applied to the eight _military expeditions_ organized from the 11th Century to the 13th, under the banner of the pagan Cross of Roman Catholicism, for the recovery of the Holy Land from the hands of the Saracens. Perhaps Billy Graham's *Global Mission 1995 Crusade*, on _March 16th, 17th and 18th_, and his "*Protestant Military Expeditions*" over the years have had something to do with the Pope's visit to Israel in 2000? In ancient Rome, the festivals in **_March_** inaugurated the _military campaign._ On March 14, (*Equirria*), March 17, (*Agonium Martiale*), March 19, (*Quinquatrus*) and March 23,

(Tubilustrium). These feasts have long been dedicated to the *capture of Israel* and the destruction of the enemies of the Roman State. *Both* Billy Graham's *Global Mission '95*, on *March 16th, 17th and 18th,* and Pope John Paul II's six-day visit to Israel, on *March 21 - 26, 2000*, were Satanically synchronized to these very dates! Hollywood's Academy *"Oscar"*Awards on *March 25, 2001*, are the same! [Old English *Osgar*, compound of *os* 'a god' and *gar* 'spear' simply is another term for *Caesar*. Remember? 'Caesar' Etruscan *aesar* 'a god.' The *Oscars* are gold statuettes of a Roman, *"military Sun-god-man*!"

Throughout Billy's damning autobiography are countless photos revealing his *friendship with the leaders of the world* - John F. Kennedy, Indira Ganghi, Golda Mier, Margaret Thatcher, Chinese Premier Li Peng, Lyndon Johnson, Ronald Reagan, Gerald Ford, Jimmy Carter, George Bush, Her Majesty Queen Elizabeth II, Pope John Paul II, Boris Yeltsin, Mikhail Gorbachev, President Bill Clinton and others. Didn't the Jews accuse Jesus of *not* being Caesar's friend? Didn't the chief priests say: *"we have no king but Caesar?"* (John 19:12-15).

Didn't James warn: *"whosoever therefore will be a friend of the world is the enemy of God."* (James 4:4).

Clinton Chronicles

In the film *Gladiator*, Commodus murders his father, then tells the people his father died of "natural causes." Interestingly, this old Roman habit of calling murder, "death from natural causes," seems to be a characteristic that is reminiscent of current U.S. presidents.

From the time of Bill Clinton's term as Governor of Arkansas to the end of his term as President, a large number of individuals privy to his nefarious activities have mysteriously died of suicide or "natural causes" or inexplicably gone missing. Many informed Americans believe as many as 90 to 100 people have been executed and can be included in the category of those who have died in "extremely suspicious" circumstances. Regrettably, I do not have the full list, but only a list of the most publicized ones. However, the few that I do have paint an amazing picture. When the *dates* of their deaths are put under the microscope, the results prove *"every" single one has been murdered in Satanic witchcraft ritual.* This fact irrefutably proves, beyond the slightest doubt, all these individuals have been plainly murdered—and that by *one single* initiator. Bill Clinton may 'claim' to be a good Baptist, but the truth is, *he is a multiple murderer*!

✦ Dan Casolaro died August 10, 1991, (New Moon August 10, 1991)

✦ Victor Raiser & Son died July 30, 1992, (New Moon July 29, 1992)

✦ W. Barkley / B. Hassey / S. Reynolds / T. Sabel [Clinton bodyguards] died May 19, 1993, (New Moon May 21, 1993)

✦ John A. Wilson died May 19, 1993, (New Moon May 21, 1993)

✦ Paul Wilcher died June 22, 1993, (New Moon June 20, 1993)

✦ Vincent Foster Jnr died July 20, 1993, (New Moon July 19, 1993)

✦ Jon Walker died August 15, 1993, (New Moon August 17, 1993)

- ✦ S. Heard / S. Dickson died September 10, 1993, (New Moon September 16, 1993)
- ✦ Kathy Fergusson died May 11, 1994, (New Moon May 10, 1994)
- ✦ Bill Shelton died June 12, 1994, (New Moon June 9, 1994)
- ✦ Kevin Ives / Don Henry died August 23, 1987, (New Moon August 24, 1987)
- ✦ Example: In the *Clinton Chronicles* videotape, produced by Jeremiah Films, Mrs Ives claimed her 17 year old son, Kevin Ives, and his 16 year old friend, Don Henry, accidentally discovered something to do with Clinton's drug dealing at a remote airstrip. She claims they were murdered by Bill Clinton. The police claim they were run over by a train in a remote corner of Saline County.

Obviously, because of other circumstances or events beyond the initiator's control, there will be exceptions. However, the overriding fact remains, the Devil works to a *very precise* timetable. The tragic fact is, the vast majority of people are entirely oblivious of this phenomenon.

Satan and his Astrologers

Hiroshima and Nagasaki were bombed by Satanists over the New Moon on August 8, 1945. East Germany was founded on the Full Moon/Solar Eclipse of October 7, 1949, and ceased to exist on the Full Moon of October 4, 1990 (actual date of unification was October 3). Pope John Paul II was elected head of the Roman Catholic

Church on the Full Moon of October 16, 1978. This pitiful saga rolls on and on. One could fill a book! President George Bush began the "countdown" to attack Iraq on the Full Moon of January 1, 1991, and concluded it on the New Moon of January 15, 1991. The Gulf War began on the following day January 16, 1991. In Billy Graham's autobiography *Just as I Am*, page 680, is a photograph of himself with President and Mrs. Bush on that *very* night. The inscription on the photo reads, "Billy—Thank you for being with us at this critical moment in world history—Geo Bush, January 16, 1991, 7.30 p.m."

Dear reader, the Satanic 'observance of times' (Deuteronomy 18:10-14) and 'astrology' followed by these people is pure witchcraft. **These are *not* characteristics associated with '*genuine*' Christians!**

Conclusion

On December 4, 2000, *Gladiator* was released on video in New Zealand. Two days later, on December 6, 2000, the *New Zealand Herald* published an article entitled, '*It's all Greek to them.*' Here are some extracts from what it said:

"Hollywood is turning to ancient Greek classics for inspiration as a new wave of violent action movies hits the screens. They are the new screenwriters Hollywood is desperate to use. And soon they will be at a cinema near you: Euripides, Herodotus, Homer and Aristophanes.

The classics are back—not pseudo, sword-and-sandal sagas like *Gladiator*, but the real thing. Next year *The Bacchae*, a full-length version of Euripides' sexually explicit and brutal play, will reach the screen. Produced by Hollywood film-house Turman-Morrissey, the script has been described by reviewers as "very adult." "*This is not a period piece but a movie that some will find offensive and many will find controversial.*"

In 90 action-packed minutes, a man is torn to shreds by a group of libidinous naked women, a pregnant mother is zapped by a lightning bolt sent by the father, Zeus, and, amid scenes of mass nudity, *Dionysus, the hero*, smashes his way through walls.

Scriptwriters are drawing heavily on original Greek accounts, particularly those of Herodotus, traditionally seen as the father of history. The part of Leonidas, the leader of the Spartans, is rumoured to have been written with George Clooney in mind. Mann has commissioned a second script about Julius Caesar and Pompey, whose rivalry led to civil war. Tom Hanks name has been linked to the role of Caesar.

Even the producers of *Tantalus*, a 10-hour stage epic drawn from fragments of ancient texts, have been approached by American and British producers. Mark Cousins, the BBC2 TV film critic, believes the trend represents a search for a new kind of masculinity on the screen. "As Schwarzenegger and Stallone age, there is the need for a new macho hero. It was something that started with Russell Crowe in *Gladiator*.

There are other political, motivations. "By going back to the classics, film makers can say, as they always have, 'What do you mean, we are too violent?' These early stories were just as bad. It is a less controversial way of dealing with censorship," Cousins said.]

Starting with *Gladiator*, these desperately evil films are recreating the cruelty, depravity and surging decadence of ancient Greece and Rome. Like Goebbel's "historical films" in Nazi Germany, their principal theme is the same: "Out of chaos"—a one world Satanic leader! On January 29, 2001, at the British Embassy in Washington, (Sir) Steven Spielberg received his British knighthood. Hence, he was officially received into the Queen's "inner circle." Like so many others, a great American patriot indeed. Are not people like Spielberg modern-day Hollywood "*hauspices*" of Jupiter—servants of the British sovereign?

Unquestionably, these devilish films, created by men like Spielberg, herald a time of *great persecution* soon to come for Jews and Christians.

From the time Marcus Aurelius (George Bush Snr) illegally appointed his evil son Commodus (George Bush Jnr) emperor, in the Capitol (Temple of Jupiter), in Rome (Washington D.C.), almost immediately, a crisis started to develop. When he commenced his rule, he resolutely absolved himself from his obligations as leader, and passed his imperial responsibilities on to his favourites. Like Commodus, these individuals too, were corrupt and evil. Soon a massive crisis developed. In fear of their lives (and pockets), the gutless Senate did nothing. There was a famine. The Imperial Treasury collapsed. There was a state of civil emergency throughout the empire. The decline and fall of the mighty Roman Empire had commenced, from which she would not recover.

Yet, in all this, while Rome was collapsing around him on all sides, the lascivious Commodus still persisted in his debauchery at the Colosseum. He became a laughing stock and a derision, but never relented murdering enemies of the State and Christians in the arena, (the altar of

Jupiter)—or sacrificing still others, on the Petra Scelerata, near the giant stadium!

Current events in the Middle East—the swearing in of George (Commodus) Bush Jnr on January 20, 2001, in the Capitol—the imminent deluge of classic films of brutality and wanton evil just around the corner (that will promote gladiatorial sports in our stadiums)—political leaders who are liars, cheats, thieves, murderers and paedophiles—child sacrifice and human blood drinking in the Church—"spiritual wickedness in high places" all around the world (Eph.6:12)—Satanist ministers who are "transformed as ministers of righteousness" (2 Cor.11:13-15) and a luke-warm congregation in a modern Laodicean Church...

Are not these the signs the former great *Protestant* nations are now ripe for **Judgement?**

> *"For it is impossible for those who were once*
> *enlightened, and have tasted of the heavenly gift, and*
> *were partakers of the Holy Ghost, And have tasted the*
> *good word of God, and the powers of the world to come,*
> *If they shall fall away, to renew them again unto*
> *repentance; seeing they crucify to themselves the Son of*
> *God afresh, and put him to an open shame.* (Hebrews
> 6:4-6).

In the words of William Tyndale, while he was burning at the stake:

"Lord! Open the King of England's eyes."

Dear brethren, pray for them. Even so, come, Lord Jesus.

CHAPTER FOURTEEN

LAST DAYS ALERT: GLADIATOR FIGHTS AND CHRISTIAN MARTYRDOM TO RETURN?

In this book I have outlined how Nazi leader Joseph Goebbels' propaganda was cunningly used in the production of the movie *Gladiator*. In the dedication I wrote:

> "To the martyrs of Christ in the future who may very well close the Christian era with their own blood, like their early Church brethren who opened it at its epoch, on the sands of their own local Roman sports stadiums."

Some have questioned my allegations, or denied them completely, in spite of resounding evidence to the contrary. One naïve Christian woman even had the audacity to say to me, "All these things might happen in another 50 years time—but not now!" Whether she was just plain ignorant or was suffering from denial may be open to conjecture. However, her contempt of the empirical facts is now overwhelmingly symptomatic of the _entire_ apostate Christian Church.

More recent events demonstrate the power of what I have reported. For example, in the _New Zealand Herald_, May 15, 2001, page B2, was an article entitled _"The Empire's Fights Are Back."_ The newspaper reported: "Gladiator fights, chariot races, and the torturing of Christian slaves in a lion-filled arena are poised for a comeback." "The multimillion-US-dollar venture will open on June 1 after a secretive four-year programme.

In May, 2001, the _Gladiator, limited edition, box set_ was released for sale in New Zealand. In the set is a video of the movie, _Gladiator_ and a one-hour special edition documentary about the making of _Gladiator_, called _Blood, Sand and Celluloid._ Also enclosed is a slide photo of Maximus and a CD of the film's music.

Also in the set is a 160-page book about the movie, called _Gladiator—The Making of the Ridley Scott Epic._ In the book, page 120, are the following shocking words:

> "Ridley Scott wanted (Roman Emperor) Commodus's
> grand entrance into Rome to echo Nazi-era propaganda
> films like Leni Reifenstahl's 'Triumph of the Will'.

Really? How much plainer can you get? On top of this, it just so happens that _Gladiator_ director Ridley Scott is a graduate of London's Royal College of Art and began his directing career at the BBC before moving into features. The statements and references to Leni Reifenstahl's _Triumph of the Will_ used by Ridley Scott in the film, were actually taken from BBC television's production, *Goebbels—Master of Propaganda (1994)*. This is the very same production I refer to in this book! Ridley Scott, in my opinion, knows precisely what he is doing!

Another Ridley Scott-directed film now presently showing is *HANNIBAL*. In this movie, Ridley Scott's ideas become a lot more clear. The main character, the cannibalistic Dr. Hannibal Lector, eats human flesh. The film concludes with Hannibal using a surgeon's knife, cutting off what I believe is a representation of a Jewish/Roman Catholic *SKULL CAP* from the FBI agent's (Clarice Starling) head, slicing up the FBI Agent's brains, frying them and giving them back to the still alive officer to eat.

Dear reader, do you know what this all means? What is happening is that *"The British Empire is Striking Back"* at America, the FBI, apostate Christendom, Catholicism and Judaism. Until very recently, the head of the FBI was Roman Catholic, Louis Freeh. With the appointment of George W. Bush as president, the FBI is going to come under mortal attack, as is the new U.S. President. George W. Bush is to become a type of Commodus, the laughing-stock of Rome.

The FBI AGENT in *Hannibal* will be like the American President, who thought he was smart, but ended up caricatured as a *BRAINLESS IDIOT!*

In this book, I explained how Constantine's mother was Welch, daughter of Coelgodebog, Earl of *GLOUCESTER*, and Lucius, the Welsh king, was the first king in the world to become a Christian. It is no coincidence that Prince Charles, Prince of Wales, has given a royal award to witchcraft author, J.K. Rowling, for writing the mammoth bestselling HARRY POTTER books.

Is it a coincidence that this same GLOUCESTER
CATHEDRAL signed a contract with Warner Brothers
to make the Harry Potter movie in its sanctuary, which
involves converting the "Christian" cathedral into
Hogwart's School of Witchcraft and Wizardry? Is it also
a coincidence that the Harry Potter movie is going to be
released at the end of the year 2001, head-to-head with
occultist J.R.R. Tolkien's 'Lord of the Rings' trilogy?
The first Tolkien film, *The Fellowship of the Ring*, filmed
in New Zealand, is about the struggle between good and
evil in a world of magic and lore, with Middle Earth
inhabited by man, Hobbits, Elves, Dwarfs, and wizards.
Two of Tolkien's books presently for sale in bookstores
have a picture of the Millennium Dome's *'Lion King'*
ceremony, and the <u>*PERGAMON ALTAR*</u> <u>rock</u> is on the
cover.

Now to Lucius, said to be the first king to become
a Christian. There is a brass plate in the <u>Church of St.</u>
<u>Peter on Cornhill</u> in the heart of the City of London
Corporation claiming that LUCIUS was the first Christian
King in Britian—that he founded the Church of St. Peter
on Cornhill which was the first Christian church in
London. The plate says Lucius was crowned king in
124 A.D. He is said to be buried (after some chronicles)
at London and (after some chronicles) at <u>Gloucester</u>.

It is not without significance that Gloucester Cathedral
has been turned into a school of witchcraft for the
production of the *Harry Potter* film. Of still greater
significance is the fact that the Church of St. Peter on
Cornhill, founded by Lucius, is a short walk to the City
of London Corporation Mansion House. According to
one source, the Mansion House is now the principal site
of regular witchcraft rituals in the City of London

Corporation involving the satanic, human blood sacrifice of small children.

And believe it or not, there are actually deluded, professing "Christians" who believe we've got at least 50 years to go before anything apocalyptic is likely to happen. May the Lord have mercy on us all!

REFERENCES

1. All Scriptural Quotations: KING JAMES BIBLE 1611

2. *A History of Rome* by A.F. Giles, published by T.C. Jack, 1914

3. *Fox's Book of Martyrs* by John Fox, published by Zondervan, 1967

4. *Fragen an die deutsche Geschichte (Questions on German History)* published by German Bundestag Publications, Bonn, 1992

5. *History of the Welsh Baptists 63-1770 A.D.* by J. Davis, published by D.M. Hogan, 1835

6. *Prince Charles* by Anna Sproule, published by Macmillan London Ltd., 1975

7. *Prince Charles - The Sustainable Prince* by Joan Veon, published by Hearthstone Publishing Ltd, 1997, Box 815, Oklahoma City, OK 73101.

8. *Roman and European Mythologies* by Yves Bonnefoy and Wendy Doniger, published by University of Chicago Press, 1991

9. *Roman History Literature and Antiquities* by A. Petrie, published by Oxford University Press, 1918

10. *Roman Mythology* by Stewart Perowne, published by Hamlyn Publishing, 1983

11. *Royal Heraldry - Beasts and Badges of Britain* by J.P. Brooke-Little, published by Pilgrim Press Ltd., 1987

12. *Saint George* by E.O. Gordon, published by Artison, 1989

13. *The March of Civilisation* by George Guest, published by G. Bell & Sons Ltd., 1957

14. *The Martyrs of the Coliseum* by A.J. O'Reilly, published by D. & J. Sadlier & Co., 1885

15. *The Oxford Dictionary of Christian Names* by E.G. Withycombe, published by Oxford University Press, 1977

16. *The Prince and the Paranormal* by John Dale, published by W.H. Allen & Co. Plc., 1986

17. *The Roman Empire* by M.P. Charlesworth, published by Oxford University Press, 1951

18. *The Royal House of Britain an Enduring Dynasty* by W.M.H. Milner, published by The Covenant Publishing Co., London, 1902

19. *The Two Babylons* by A. Hislop, published by Loizeax Bros., 1959

20. *Television Production, Goebbels - Master of Propaganda*, BBC, 1994

21. *We, The People* published by the U.S. Capitol Historical Society 1962

22. *100 Great Kings, Queens & Rulers of the World* by J. Canning, published by Century Books Ltd., 1973

OTHER BOOKS BY RIVERCREST

Letters on Freemasonry, *by John Quincy Adams*

Honoring the King James Bible, *by Dr. Solomon Aordkian*

Best of Bible Pathways, *edited by Dr. John Hash*

Days of Hunger, Days of Chaos, *by Texe Marrs*

Project L.U.C.I.D.: The Beast 666 Universal Human
   Control System, *by Texe Marrs*

Circle of Intrigue: The Hidden Inner Circle of the Global
   Illuminati Conspiracy, *by Texe Marrs*

Big Sister is Watching You: Hillary Clinton and the White
   House Feminists Who Now Control America—And Tell
   the President What to Do, *by Texe Marrs*

Dark Majesty: The Secret Brotherhood and the Magic of A
   Thousand Points of Light, *by Texe Marrs*

Millennium: Peace, Promises, and the Day They Take Our
   Money Away, *by Texe Marrs*

America Shattered, *by Texe Marrs*

New Age Cults and Religions, *by Texe Marrs*

Mystery Mark of the New Age, *by Texe Marrs*

Dark Secrets of the New Age, *by Texe Marrs*

New Age Lies to Women, *by Wanda Marrs*

FOR MORE INFORMATION

For a complete catalog of books, tapes, and videos about the occult, bible prophecy, conspiracy and related topics, and a free sample newsletter, please phone toll-free: 1-800-234-9673, or write to:

RiverCrest Publishing
1708 Patterson Road
Austin, Texas 78733

For additional information we highly recommend
the following websites:

www.powerofprophecy.com
www.conspiracyworld.com

MYSTERY SCANDAL COVERUPS

WELCOME TO CONSPIRACYWORLD.COM

Your One Resource to the Whole Universe of Conspiracy, Mystery, Scandal, Intrigue, Coverups, And the Unexplained!

CLICK ON YOUR TOPIC OF INTEREST
UNCOVER THE MYSTERY, SCANDAL, AND CONSPIRACY

Satanism, Occult, Black Magic Arts
Deaths and Assassinations
Secret Societies and Orders
Goverment and Big Brother Police State
Environmentalism
UFOs, Aliens, Extraterrestrials
Illness, Disease, Genocide, and Depopulatio
Biblical Mysteries and Science
Codex Magica-Hidden Codes and Symbols
Mind Control and Black Science
Illuminati and Globalism
Vatican
Mysteries and the Unexplained
Money and Banking
Mysterious Monuments and Secret Architecture
Space and Other Worlds
Witchcraft, Goddess, Pagans
Zionism and Israel
Numerology and Mathematics
Hollywood, Entertainment, Celebrities
New Age and Astrology
Hoaxes and Scams
Religion, Prophecy, Cults
Political and Politicians
Technology and Computers

HOT FEATURES!

- Test Your Conspiracy IQ
- Texe Marrs, Our Founder
- Thinker's Quote
- Breaking News!!!
- Black Boot Award
- Hot Product of the Month
- Newest Bestseller List
- Free Gift
- What *The New York Times* Said About Texe Marrs
- Texe Marrs' Intelligence Examiner™

BOOKMARK US:
Hold down the ctrl key and press D to add Conspiracyworld.com
to your browser's favorites.

WE OFFER:
The Best in Conspiracy related books, audiotapes, and videos.

- Shop With Confidence
- Safe, Reliable Ordering
- Your Privacy Always Protected

conspiracyworld.com

Your *One Resource* to the
whole universe of conspiracy,
coverup, mystery, scandals,
and the unexplained.